Martha Stewart's

Grilling

Martha Stewart's

Grilling

125+ Recipes for Gatherings Large and Small

From the Kitchens of Martha Stewart Living
Photographs by Elizabeth Cecil and others

Clarkson Potter/Publishers
New York

Published in the United States by Clarkson Potter/Publishers, an imprint
of the Crown Publishing Group, a division of Random House LLC, a
Penguin Random House Company, New York.
crownpublishing.com
clarksonpotter.com
marthastewart.com

CLARKSON POTTER is a trademark and POTTER with colophon is a
registered trademark of Penguin Random House LLC.

Library of Congress Cataloging-in-Publication Data
is available upon request.

ISBN 978-1-524-763374
Ebook ISBN 978-1-5247-6337-4

Printed in China

Book design by Michele Outland
Photographs by Elizabeth Cecil and others
Cover photograph by Marcus Nilsson
Complete photograph credits appear on page 248.

10 9 8 7 6 5 4 3 2 1

First Edition

To everyone who enjoys getting outside to prepare meats
and fish and vegetables over an open fire

Contents

Recipes 8

Introduction 13

The Basics 14

At the Start 35

As a Main 77

Out of Hand 113

On a Platter 155

On the Side 189

At the End 213

Sauces, Marinades, and More 237

Photograph Credits 248

Acknowledgments 248

Index 250

Recipes

At the Start

Honey-Brined Chicken Wings   37

Kielbasa Bites with Potato Salad   38

Italian Sausages and Tomatoes on Focaccia   41

Kofta Kebabs   42

Shrimp with Cilantro, Lime, and Peanuts   45

Grilled Oysters with Fennel-Shallot Butter   46

Grilled Fresh Sardines with Crostini   49

Shishito Peppers and Chorizo   50

Red-Curry Salmon Bites   53

Charred Okra with Paprika and Fresh Thyme   54

Chicken Satay   57

Grilled Spring Vegetables with Almond Aïoli and Anchoïade   58

Grilled Vegetable Antipasto   61

Grilled Bread and Chiles with Burrata Cheese   62

Grilled Peaches and Figs with Prosciutto and Robiola   65

Bourbon Mint Tea   69

Basil French 75   69

Upside-Down Martini   69

Americano   69

Lime Shandy   70

Lemon Shandy   70

Cherry Beer   70

Sherry-Sangria   73

Sparkling Rosé Sangria   73

White Sangria   73

Jasmine Tea and Orange Juice   74

Chamomile Tea and Limeade   74

Rooibos Tea and Grapefruit   74

As a Main

Chicken with Green Chile Dressing   78

Lemon-Herb Spatchcocked Chicken   81

Buttermilk-and-Rosemary Brined Chicken   82

Chicken and Vegetable Kebabs   85

Peppercorn-Brined Pork Chops   86

Pork and Chorizo Kebabs   89

Lamb Shoulder Chops with Herb Aïoli   90

Leg of Lamb with Garlic and Mint   93

Rib-Eye with Jalapeño Butter   94

Balsamic-Marinated Hanger Steak   97

Sirloin and Vegetable Kebabs   98

Salmon Fillets with Orange-Herb Butter   101

Swordfish with Sicilian Oregano-Caper Sauce   102

Sweet and Spicy Grilled Shrimp   105

Grilled Whole Fish with Two Herb Fillings   106

Grilled Lobster with Mixed Herb Sauce   109

Tofu with Ginger-Cilantro Sauce   110

Out of Hand

Steakhouse Burgers   114

Martha's Favorite Cheeseburgers   117

Turkey-and-Bacon Burgers   118

All-Time Favorite Turkey Burgers   121

Chickpea and Lamb Sliders   122

Smoked-Brisket Sandwiches   124

Lemongrass Pork Burgers in Lettuce
   Cups   128

Classic Pulled Pork Sandwiches   131

Grilled Ribs with Tangy Barbecue
   Sauce   132

Bistro-Style Chicken Sandwiches   135

Steak and Charred-Tomato
   Sandwiches   136

New England Fish Sandwiches   139

Salmon Sandwiches with Herbed
   Mayonnaise   140

Tofu Bánh Mì   143

Chile-Rubbed Flank Steak Tacos   144

Fish Tacos with Shredded Cabbage   147

Grilled Pork Tacos al Pastor   148

Fire-Roasted Rajas Tacos with Beans   151

Korean Short Ribs   152

On a Platter

Chicken and Pea Salad with Dijon
   Vinaigrette   156

Grilled Chicken and Sausage with Leeks,
   Shallots, and Onions   159

Chicken with Cucumber, Radish, and
   Cherry Tomato Relish   160

Citrus-Chile Turkey Breast   163

Ginger-Soy Pork Chops with Bok
   Choy   164

Porterhouse Steaks with Paprika Potatoes
   and Lemony Romaine Wedges   167

Honey-Glazed Pork Tenderloin with Grilled
   Apricots   168

Sirloin Skewers with Zucchini, Mint,
   and Rice   171

Lamb Kebabs with Naan, Cilantro Chutney,
   and Raita   172

Salmon Salad with Sugar Snap Peas, Eggs,
   and Potatoes   175

Striped Bass with Clam Chowder   176

Caesar Salad with Mojo-Marinated
   Shrimp   179

Sea Scallops over Shallot-Herb Pasta   180

Whole Fish with Potatoes, Chiles, and
   Fennel   183

Grilled Halloumi Cheese and Vegetables
   with Smoky-Tomato Dressing   185

Soba Salad with Grilled Eggplant and
   Tomato   186

On the Side

Watermelon, Orange, and Feta Salad   190

Potato and Green Bean Salad   193

Grilled Kale and Radicchio with Balsamic-
    Orange Glaze   194

Peach Panzanella   197

Grilled Corn, Mint, and Scallion
    Salad   198

Baby Bok Choy Slaw   200

Cabbage and Radish Slaw with
    Peanut Dressing   201

Farro with Zucchini, Pine Nuts, and
    Lemon Zest   205

Sardinian Tomato Salad   206

Grilled Ratatouille and Bulgur Salad   209

Grilled Romaine and Radicchio with
    Polenta Croutons   210

At the End

Iced Cocoa Pops   214

Berry Fizz Float   217

Peach Sherbet and Sorbet   218

Brownie Sundae Ice-Cream Cake   220

Lime Curd   224

Vanilla-Bourbon Butterscotch   224

Hot Fudge Sauce   224

Fresh-Strawberry Sauce   224

Grilled Pound Cake with Seasonal Fruit   227

Watermelon Campari Granita   229

Lemon and Mint Granita   229

Grilled Stone-Fruit Fool   230

Summer-Fruit Cream Pie   232

Sauces, Marinades, and More   237

Tahini Sauce

Tapenade

Chimichurri

Rouille

Yogurt-Cucumber
    Sauce

Chopped-Chile
    Relish

Lebanese Tomato
    Sauce

Aïoli

Salsa Verde

Romesco

Almond Aïoli

Anchoïade

Cucumber Raita

Cilantro Chutney
    with Coconut
    and Lime

Caesar Dressing

Smoky Chipotle
    Salsa

Coleslaw

Pickled Vegetables

Tangy Barbecue
    Sauce

All-Purpose
    Barbecue Sauce

All-Purpose Rub

All-Purpose
    Marinade

All-Purpose Dry
    Brine

Pound Cake

Gingered Nuts

Introduction

I admit that before working on this book, I was not an avid griller. I am no Bobby Flay and certainly not a Francis Mallmann. I never appreciated the smoke, nor the strong flavors of mesquite or charcoal, and I certainly didn't appreciate charred or blackened meats. But once we began working on this book, and I started to experiment with various grills—the Argentine *parrilla*, the "egg," the "dome," the smoker, the gas-fired, the wood-fired, the campfire— I began to see the variety one can attain in flavors, and the unique timing and simplicity of cooking out in the open, away from the confines of a household kitchen.

Some of this book was photographed on the rooftop terrace of our office complex on West 26th Street in New York City, some of it on Long Island and in Brooklyn. We know from experience that these recipes work on a variety of grills. And we know they all taste very good, because we tested and tasted each one of them, and made them with readily available, fresh ingredients.

I spend a lot of time in Maine, where we now cook outdoors quite frequently. We roast corn, create massive paellas over wood fires, and carefully grill halves of lobsters, their sweet flesh bathed in tasty beurre blanc or herb sauce. We roast oysters and clams, grill pizzas, and, when the mood strikes, toss on some burgers and franks for an old-fashioned American cookout.

The techniques for grilling are few, but they should be taken seriously if you want the results to be A-plus. Make the perfect fire, have the temperature of the coals exactly right, prepare the food to be grilled meticulously, and get to work! You will find grilling to be fun, the food delicious. And remember, treat the meats and fish gingerly—no pressing, no compacting, no turning before one side is done!

Martha Stewart

The Basics

At Martha Stewart Living, we love to entertain outdoors, and there is no better way to do that than to fire up the grill. It provides us with a welcoming sense of freedom, as we leave the confines of our kitchens, and invites community and conviviality, as family and friends gather around to sip cold drinks and share a meal and some good conversation.

Beyond the flavor and the camaraderie of grilling, it also offers a challenge. Unlike most cooking techniques, such as sautéing and roasting, grilling involves flames directly meeting ingredients. Mastering a live fire provides a cook with a unique feeling of satisfaction and conquering the elements. This is a book to help you in that mastery; to expand your skills if you're already experienced; and, if you're new to the grill, to introduce you to its pleasures. From grill to table, we'll guide you along the way, with the hope that you come to enjoy grilling as much as we do.

In the pages that follow, we've collected longtime favorites and new dishes alike—from starters through desserts—to inspire you and to satisfy all your menu needs. We'll show you different techniques for both charcoal and gas grills, how to prep ingredients to simplify entertaining, and the best ways to showcase grilled food. You'll find signature cocktails and appetizers to crave

in At the Start; no-utensils-required burgers, tacos, and kebabs in Out of Hand; our favorite back-pocket recipes in As a Main; one-stop dishes for a small group in On a Platter; accompaniments for every barbecue in On the Side; and sweets that are either grilled or chilled in At the End.

Grilling is international—every culture cooks over fire—and these recipes reflect that. Our best meaty burgers join a Middle Eastern chickpea version, and a classic Southern pulled pork sandwich meets up with Mexican pork tacos al pastor. Korean-style short ribs and mojo-marinated shrimp are side by side with grilled whole lobster and balsamic-marinated steak. There are kofta kebabs and honey-soy pork chops; chilled soba noodles and a Sardinian tomato salad. Desserts of fruit cream pie and brownie sundae ice-cream cake keep the fun, simple spirit of the cookout going. Of course, it all begins when you have a few basic guidelines and just get grilling.

The Golden Rules

Prioritize Safety

Position the grill at least ten feet away from anything that could catch fire. Remove excess fat and marinade from food to reduce flare-ups; if they occur, transfer food to a safe zone (an open, unheated area of the grill). If they continue, turn the burner(s) off—never try to put them out with water. Wait 24 hours to dispose of ash. Finally, it's good practice to keep a fire extinguisher nearby.

Be Prepared

Meat, poultry, and whole fish will cook more evenly if you bring them to room temperature before placing them on the grill. Fish fillets and shellfish should be kept cold to stay fresh.

Bring all essential tools to the grill, so you can tend the fire once it is lit. Always transfer cooked foods from the grill to a clean platter; never use the platter on which you transported raw meat.

Brush Up on Cleaning

Get in the routine of cleaning the grates before *and* after cooking. It's easier when the grill is warm: Using a wire grill brush, scrape the grates of a preheated grill before cooking, then again after you are finished. See "Cleaning the Grill" (page 33).

Oil the Grates

To keep food from sticking, use a heatproof silicone brush to coat the grate with vegetable oil—it's inexpensive and does the trick (or rub the grate with an oiled rag or paper towels held with tongs). Apply the oil just before you place the food on the grill; otherwise, it may burn off before you start cooking.

Know Your Zones

The key to success, whether with a gas or a charcoal grill, often involves creating two zones: one for high, direct heat and another for low, indirect heat. Choose direct heat (placing the food directly over the flame) for tender, smaller cuts such as burgers, steaks, kebabs, and fish. Indirect heat allows for a medium-low temperature that lets you cook large items through without burning the outside. Use indirect heat when you want to cook large pieces, such as a whole chicken or bone-in parts, turkey breast, pork shoulder, brisket, or leg of lamb. (For more, see "How to Light a Fire for Grilling," page 22.)

Don't Crowd the Grill

Keep some space between items so everything cooks evenly. Leave a safe zone, where food can be moved in the event of a flare-up.

Choose Your Grill

The grilling world can be divided into two general camps: people who value the convenience of a gas appliance versus purists who prefer the authentic taste charcoal imparts. Before deciding which grill is best for you, consider what kind of cook you are. If you grill often and prefer the ease of an appliance that ignites with the flip of a switch, a gas grill may be best. If the smell of charcoal and the crackle of fire lift your spirits, consider a classic kettle-style grill. Or you may discover that just one grill won't do, and opt for a gas grill for weekdays when you're busy and a charcoal grill on the weekends, when your schedule is more relaxed. Some gas grills can even convert to charcoal operations with the addition of a tray that holds the charcoal beneath the grates. Knowing some advantages and disadvantages of each type will help you make your decision.

Charcoal Grills

There are a lot of rewards from cooking with charcoal. Foremost, there is nothing like the distinct flavor that results from the fat of a sizzling steak or herbs from a marinade dripping onto white-hot charcoal, causing aromatic smoke to envelop the food. And though there's more to building a charcoal fire than the simple knob-turning that a gas grill requires, using a chimney starter (see page 22) makes firing up the coals easy and efficient.

Most charcoal grills are freestanding, with the classic Weber kettle grill, which focuses heat, being the most popular. Look for a kettle made of high-grade steel, with high sides to shield flames from the wind. Double walls, which some grills offer, provide extra heat retention. The ceramic, inch-thick walls of charcoal grills like the *kamado*, including the Big Green Egg and Kamado Joe brands, allow for higher surface temperatures (they can get up to 300 degrees hotter than a traditional kettle grill) and are therefore terrific for searing steaks or cooking whole chicken.

When considering which size to choose, think about how often you grill, on what occasions, and for how many people. It's important that the grill surface allows you to create two heat zones, such as indirect and direct, without crowding the food in either area. The standard size for a kettle grill is 22 inches in diameter; if you're going to regularly feed a large crowd, you can opt for a 37-inch model.

Gas Grills

A gas model offers ease and convenience plus plenty of optional amenities, including warming drawers and side burners for steaming and boiling. Powered by propane tanks or piped-in natural gas, these grills feature a barrier, such as lava rock or steel plates, between the flame and cooking grate for dispersing the heat. When cooking, juices from the food hit the barrier and create flavorful smoke. Some experts say this can't compare with infusing food with charcoal smoke. However, the ability to control temperature and the even heat that a gas grill offers are big pluses.

Gas grills are sold according to their rating in BTUs (British thermal units), which are used to measure the grill's heat output. In general, a model should have about 100 BTUs per square inch of cooking surface. But don't judge a grill only on this number: The efficiency of the grill in maintaining the heat is more important, and some models are constructed in a way that allows them to reach a favorable cooking temperature using fewer BTUs.

Choose a gas grill made of heavy-gauge stainless steel or cast aluminum; both are more sturdy and rust-resistant than sheet metal or lower-quality stainless steel, and facilitate the flow of hot air inside. Grates should be heavy-duty as well. Two or more burners are preferable (most people want four) as this allows you to heat large items evenly or cook foods at different temperatures. Infrared burners can heat to more than 1,000 degrees and are your best bet for a quick sear. Sizes range from about 350 square inches to about 550 square inches (you can fit more than 25 burgers on these large grills). Many companies sell the top portions of their freestanding gas grills—the cooking surfaces and heat mechanisms—for use as built-ins for outdoor kitchens.

Portable Grill

Portable grills are a smart choice if you have a small backyard, grill only a couple of times a year, or want to take it on the go.

The definitive portable grill is the charcoal hibachi, a frills-free, lidless grill that uses charcoal to produce a powerful heat. Because the fire is exposed to plenty of air, food cooks rapidly, which can be a plus; but you do need to watch for flare-ups. When cared for, a cast-iron hibachi should last years. Lidded travel charcoal grills, such as a compact kettle or box-style, are slightly easier to use.

If you prefer a propane-powered grill, travel models range from a small tabletop style (about 185 square inches of cooking surface) to a two-burner affair with 285 square inches of cooking space that mimics a roller suitcase, sets up on a sturdy built-in stand, and has slide-out side tables for extra prep surface. You can also find stainless-steel models with multiple grilling surfaces.

Stovetop Grill Pan

Though most of us associate grilling with warmer weather, we heartily embrace making it a year-round routine. During inclement weather, you can even achieve the smoky flavors and charred grill marks with a cast-iron grill pan. You can cook chicken, steak, vegetables, kebabs, and even fruit on a stovetop pan, and get grill marks from the ridges, which are similar to grates on a grill. Choose cast iron, which conducts heat well and cooks foods evenly. (Before using any cast-iron pan, always season it according to the manufacturer's instructions.)

Grilling with Wood

Campers know the beauty of cooking over a wood fire—a hot dog held over flames on a stick, a just-caught fish in a cast-iron pan sitting in embers, the gooey sweet s'more. Patience is the key to wood-fire cooking, as wood burns faster than charcoal, so the embers require more frequent replenishing and raking to control the heat. Many grilling fans are turning to wood, from the basic grate on a stand that sits over a fire pit to extravagantly designed grills based on ancient methods. The Argentines, who have perfected the art of grilling steak, have inspired a turn toward the *parrilla*, which in its simplest form is a cast-iron grate placed over a fire, typically angled to allow the meat juices to run into a basting pan, and to allow the food to easily be moved closer or farther from the fire. There are now many high-end options available—including stainless-steel models with fire cages, crank wheel–controlled grates, multiple grill stations, and removable rotisseries.

Glossary of Fuels

Building a fire requires starting with the right fuel, one that will maintain a strong, steady heat during your cooking process. Gas grills keep it simple— they run on a tank of liquid propane, or natural gas, which can be purchased at your local hardware or grocery store. There are a few more options to consider with a charcoal grill:

Hardwood Lump Charcoal

Made from natural hardwood, such as oak and mesquite, this charcoal burns the cleanest and hottest—although fast, too. It's our preferred fuel for the grill, as it contains no additives and provides a sustained heat.

Pressed Charcoal Briquettes

Though briquettes are easy to start and they burn at the same rate due to their uniform size and shape, they also contain additives. Along with charcoal, they contain sawdust, starch (which acts as a binder), and sodium nitrate. Because they burn fast, they also result in more ash build-up, and you will need to replenish the coals more often.

Instant Charcoal Briquettes

The simplest fuel to use, instant briquettes contain the additives mentioned above, plus chemicals such as petroleum to ease lighting. We don't recommend them, as they do not burn clean and the fumes may impart a chemical taste to food.

Wood Chips

Using wood chips can lend additional smoky flavor. Apple and cherry woods impart a sweet flavor while birch, hickory, and mesquite are more robustly smoky. Use large chunks for charcoal grills, smaller wood chips for gas. They burn hot and fast, so they should be added repeatedly throughout the grilling process in order to keep the smoke level constant. Start with one to two handfuls and replenish as needed (time will vary depending on the recipe, usually between one to two hours). Some grill aficionados believe the chips should be added dry and replaced often, while conventional wisdom says that soaking the wood chips at least 2 hours before grilling helps maintain a slow, steady smolder; this effectively lowers the temperature and adds some steam to a closed grill. Whichever method you prefer, you'll need to replace the chips, gradually, once they burn out to maintain ideal smokiness.

How to Light a Fire for Grilling

Preparing a Charcoal Grill

Building a charcoal fire is easy to master with a few simple steps.

Step 1

Prepare the chimney starter: First, remove the grill's cooking grate (the one on top). Place the chimney on the lower grate. Place a few sheets of crumpled newspaper in the bottom of the cylinder, then fill it to the brim with coals.

Step 2

Light the coals: From the bottom of the cylinder, light the newspaper in several places, which in turn will ignite the coals (A). Let them continue to burn until most flames have died down, coals are turning whitish-gray, and there's a red glow inside the chimney, about 15 minutes.

Step 3

Set up your zones for direct and indirect heat: Very carefully pour the hot coals from the chimney onto the lower grate. Use long-handled tongs to arrange them into an even layer, leaving a quarter to a third of the grate free of coal for the indirect-heat zone and banking the hot coals across the rest of the grill for the direct-heat zone (B). Alternatively, you can create one by arranging the coals around a drip pan (such as a disposable aluminum pan), with the food centered over the pan (C). Replace the top grate as soon as the fire is going, to preheat the grates. (You will need to replenish the hot coals about every hour.)

Step 4

Allow the grill to preheat for about 10 minutes before cleaning the cooking grates. Scrub the hot grates briskly with a steel- or brass-bristled brush to remove charred debris and residue (D). If you don't have a grill brush, crush a sheet of heavy-duty aluminum foil into a ball, grasp it with long tongs, and use it to scrub the grates.

Preparing a Gas Grill

To start a gas grill, lift the lid, open the tank valve, and turn the front or first burner to high. After two to three seconds, push the igniter. Depending on the model, you may have to turn on each burner individually. Close the lid and preheat for about 10 minutes on high. Clean the grill grates, then adjust the burners to create two zones: For direct heat, the food should be placed directly over the flame. For indirect heat, the burners should be lit on either side of the food, creating a ring of heat around it. With grills that have just two burners, there is most likely already a natural indirect-heat area between the burners. With a three-burner, turn the center burner off to create the indirect-heat zone. For a four-burner, turn the two center burners off.

An Open-and-Shut Case

There's no hard and fast rule for when you should close the lid or leave it open on your grill. Some charcoal-grill cooks almost always grill with the lid open, so it's easier to see what's happening and to better control cooking times. Meanwhile, those cooking on gas grills often keep the lid down.

That said, when slow-roasting a larger cut of meat, finishing a steak, or smoking something like a brisket or ribs, we recommend closing the lid. For example, in the initial low-and-slow stage of cooking spatch-cocked chicken over indirect heat, cover the grill to retain heat. In the last stage, for crisping and charring the skin, uncover the grill. Just remember to move the food to a cooler zone if flare-ups occur.

When grilling quick-cooking ingredients like shrimp and tender vegetables, leave the lid open to easily turn the food as it chars. This way you'll immediately know when your food is ready.

Whether you put the lid on for indirect or direct cooking, leave the vent open to allow airflow and ensure proper burning.

gauging the heat

The proper temperature of a grill is crucial. It's easy to determine the temperature of gas grills, since the burners can be controlled and many models are equipped with built-in thermometers. Charcoal grills are a bit more difficult to gauge, but simply placing your hand about 4 inches above the grate is a good measuring method. Try this handy—and easy-to-remember—way to monitor the temperature of the grill:

High (375°F to 400°F):
If you can hold your hand for only 2 to 3 full seconds (count: one-one-thousand, two-one-thousand) before it becomes uncomfortable, the heat is high.

Medium-high (350°F to 375°F):
Count 4 to 5 seconds.

Medium (300°F to 350°F):
Count 6 to 8 seconds.

Medium-low (200°F to 300°F):
Count 9 to 10 seconds.

Low (under 200°F):
Count 11 to 14 seconds.

Is It Done Yet?

Each fire is different, so learn to look for cues for doneness by watching what's on the grill while it cooks. You will begin to know when to turn, and whether you need to move things around more or less frequently, so you can achieve the beautiful grill marks or deep, brown crust that you want. (See our tips on pages 30–31 for cues.) Until you're ready to use your senses as a guide, an instant-read thermometer is the best way to check doneness. Stick the instant-read thermometer in the thickest part of the meat or fish, away from any bones—and, of course, be sure not to touch the grates of the grill. For thinner cuts, if using a thermometer, insert it through the side and into the middle, not from the top down; this is because the point on the thermometer that reads temperature is about two inches up the side. Bear in mind that the temperature of meat will continue to rise by about five degrees once it's taken off the grill. Try to anticipate this by taking the temperature often and removing meat from the grill before it hits the mark.

If cooking for young children, pregnant women, or anyone with a weakened immune system, be sure to follow the USDA-recommended guidelines for your target temperature. Otherwise, most professional kitchens recommend a few degrees lower for ideal flavor and texture. Our guidelines follow (temperatures taken before resting):

Beef: 125°F to 130°F for medium-rare (USDA recommends 145°F)

Ground beef: 160°F

Pork: 138°F to 140°F for medium (USDA recommends 145°F)

Ground pork: 160°F

Lamb: 135°F to 140°F for medium (USDA recommends 145°F)

Ground lamb: 160°F

Poultry (whole bird, thighs, legs, wings, or ground meat): 165°F

Chicken breasts: 160°F (USDA recommends 165°F)

Must-Have Tools

It's a good practice to have all your tools close at hand. Once you get that grill going, you'll need to monitor the fire. Here's a list of the essentials:

CLOCKWISE FROM TOP, OPPOSITE:
A **chimney starter** is an indispensable tool for charcoal fires.

Skewers (either metal or wooden) prove useful for kebabs, fish, vegetables, and testing for doneness. Double-pronged or flat skewers keep the food from spinning on the grill. Wooden skewers need to be soaked in water for 30 minutes before use.

A **grill brush** with sturdy brass- or steel-wire bristles helps with cleaning the grates. Most brushes come with a wooden, stainless-steel, or plastic handle, and, as with all grilling tools, a long handle is the most practical.

Metal tongs that are spring-loaded and long-handled are best for holding, lifting, flipping, and moving food during cooking. Scalloped edges provide a better grip.

A **large offset spatula** with a long, angled handle and flexible, beveled blade is great for flipping burgers and fish.

A **barbecue fork** turns large cuts of meat, but use it with restraint to avoid letting meat juices escape.

Basting brushes can be used before and during grilling; bristle brushes hold oils and sauces well, and silicone-bristled versions are easy to clean and last for years.

Grill baskets allow for easy turning of fish and batches of vegetables, preventing them from slipping into the fire.

A **lighter** or **matches** gets the grill fired up; choose long kitchen matches, a long-handled lighter, or an electric fire starter to light your charcoal.

An **instant-read thermometer** determines the temperature of meat and can aid your strategy for reaching desired doneness.

Barbecue gloves or **mitts** should be heat-resistant and nonslip to protect your hands.

Kitchen towels come in handy for wiping up spills, cleaning hands, and grabbing a hot handle. You can also use them, with long-handled tongs, to oil hot grates.

OTHER ITEMS TO HAVE ON HAND:
Rimmed baking sheets are useful for carrying food to the grill. Be sure to have another (clean!) one for cooked foods.

Parchment-lined aluminum foil can be used to loosely tent grilled meats and veggies to keep them warm before serving. Foil can also be balled up and used in place of a grill brush to scrub the grates.

A **headlamp** will shine some much-needed light when you're grilling at night.

A **fire extinguisher** should be kept nearby at all times.

Tips and Techniques

Whether you're cooking steaks or fish, understanding some basic techniques will immediately increase your confidence at the grill. Here are some tips to get you started:

Burgers

• Use quality ingredients: Custom-ground blends and a higher fat grind (such as 80% to 20% meat to fat ratio for ground chuck) and dark-meat chicken and turkey make the juiciest burgers.

• To prevent dense burgers, don't overhandle the meat: When shaping patties, don't pack the meat too tightly. Use about 6 ounces per patty, making burgers about ½ inch wider than the buns (they will shrink during cooking). Using your thumb, indent the center of each patty, so the burger holds its shape during cooking instead of puffing up in the middle.

• Keep burgers cold and salt right before grilling, not in advance.

• To keep burgers juicy, don't press patties down with a spatula during grilling.

• To prevent burgers from sticking to the grill, wait until they form a crust before moving; this is particularly beneficial to vegetable burgers, to maintain their shape.

• Follow these general guidelines for desired doneness:

Rare: Soft when prodded, and does not spring back in the center.

Medium-Rare: Still soft when prodded in center, but springier, with some firmness at the edges.

Well-Done: Springy when prodded.

Chicken

• Begin cooking bone-in chicken (parts or whole) over indirect heat. (This first phase renders the fat to avoid flare-ups.) Turn often to ensure slow, even browning. Finish over direct heat to achieve a crispy and deeply browned skin. Spatchcocking the bird (see page 81) is a way to ensure the meat cooks evenly—and fast—while also achieving an impeccably crisp skin.

• For breast pieces and most boneless chicken, position over direct heat.

• If the fire flares up, move the chicken to a cooler part of the grill. If it continues, remove chicken until flames subside.

• If using barbecue sauce, brush it on toward the end of the cooking time and again just before taking the meat off the grill—not on the raw chicken—so the sauce doesn't burn.

• When done, each piece should have crisp browned skin, and the juices should run clear when the meat is pierced.

Fish

• Whole red snapper, branzino, and striped bass all grill up nicely and make impressive presentations. For fillets, opt for firm-fleshed, sturdy fish such as salmon or bluefish. If you prefer more delicate options (like flounder or sole), buy thick pieces.

• Clean the grates well to prevent sticking.

• Use two large metal spatulas or a grill basket to keep the fish intact when turning.

• Fish will cook quickly over direct heat. Make slashes on the skin before grilling to see when the fish is done: the flesh should be opaque and flaking. You can also insert a metal skewer into the thickest part to test for doneness; the skewer should not meet resistance and should come out warm.

Steaks

• Rib-eyes and porterhouses can be a delicious splurge; skirt, flank, and hanger are more economical as well as full of flavor.

• The secret to a great steak, whatever the cut, is a very hot grill, as the heat helps the meat to form a flavorful dark-brown crust.

• Some more fibrous cuts, like skirt and flank steak, benefit from a marinade, which adds flavor.

• Start steaks over direct heat. Some thicker cuts finish over indirect heat.

• With practice, you can tell when meat is ready by touch. Prodded, a rare steak will feel soft, like the webbed area between your thumb and forefinger. Medium-rare is a bit firmer: touch the same spot but with the hand outstretched. For medium, make a fist; that part of your hand will be tighter still. (Well-done meat will spring back and can be as firm as your chin.)

• Allow steaks to rest 10 to 15 minutes after cooking—larger roasts will need at least 20 minutes. This allows the juices to redistribute and be reabsorbed throughout the meat. And slice steaks against the grain; fibrous cuts should be thinly sliced.

Bone-in Pork Chops

• Because they have a bit more fat than leaner cuts, bone-in chops won't dry out as easily when grilled. For extra-juicy chops, brine the pork first; for a simple brine recipe, see page 246.

• Grill pork chops over direct heat. When the chops are done, the exteriors should be lightly golden with grill marks. The interiors should be juicy and just barely pink.

• Let the meat sit about 5 minutes after cooking, allowing the juices to redistribute.

Tofu

• Firm tofu stands up best to grilling, so be sure to buy firm or extra-firm. Then, cut slices at least $\frac{1}{2}$ inch thick, so they won't tear as easily.

• Press the tofu to remove water: Lay cut tofu on a rimmed baking sheet lined with a double layer of paper towels. Top tofu with another double layer of paper towels and another baking sheet. Weight with a heavy skillet or canned goods to press out the excess liquid. Let stand 15 to 20 minutes, then pat the tofu dry with paper towels.

• Marinate the tofu 30 minutes before grilling, to add flavor and help keep it moist, or brush with a flavorful sauce, such as chimichurri (see page 238 for recipe).

• To achieve great grill marks, grill over direct heat, turning once, until crisp and charred in spots, about 2 minutes per side.

Cleaning the Grill

The more you use your grill, the more seasoned the grates become and the better your food tastes. Cleaning is just a matter of maintenance, and with regular care, you shouldn't need to use harsh abrasives. Avoid putting parts in the dishwasher, which could rinse away that desirable seasoning patina that develops over time.

For Gas Grills

With each use
Preheat the grill with all the burners on high for about 10 minutes. Scrub the hot grates briskly with a brass- or steel-bristle brush. (The brush itself won't need cleaning.) If you don't have a grill brush, crush a sheet of heavy-duty aluminum foil into a ball, grasp it with tongs, and use it to scrub the grates.

After grilling, close the lid and leave the burners on for about 10 minutes to burn off any food. Then turn off the heat and immediately scrub the grates again.

Check drip pans. Once a month, empty and clean the large one that catches food, if you grill often; wear rubber gloves and wash with a scrubbing sponge and dishwashing liquid. The smaller, disposable pan below the larger one catches grease. Replace it with a new aluminum pan when it is half full.

Once a year
Each year, give your grill a thorough cleaning. Turn the burners on high, close the lid, and let the grill run for 20 to 40 minutes, depending on how dirty it is. Turn the burners off when the residue has burned down to a white-gray ash that can be brushed away easily. Turn the heat off and scrub the grates thoroughly.

Let the grill cool, then disconnect the propane tank. Wearing rubber gloves, wash the lid grates and the exterior using dishwashing liquid, warm water, and a scrubbing sponge. Rinse well. Remove and wash the large drip pan, and replace the small pan.

For Charcoal Grills

With each use
Preheat the grill with the lid on but the vents open for 10 to 15 minutes. Scrub the grates with a grill brush. After cooking, scrub the grates again. Replace the lid and let the coals burn out, incinerating any leftover food. When the grill is cool, use a metal scoop to remove ashes, transferring them to a small metal pail to avoid a fire hazard.

Once a year
Wash and rinse the grill inside and out using a sudsy mix of dishwashing liquid and warm water and a scrubbing sponge. It's easy to take the grill apart and give the pieces a good rinse with a garden hose. Let the pieces dry in the sun before reassembling.

At the Start

The beauty of the grill is its ability to encourage spontaneity. This collection of light bites with festive cocktails makes that even easier, with recipes to suit any occasion. When friends drop by unexpectedly, try mixed vegetable kebabs or chicken satays—these require little preparation and you may already have most of the ingredients on hand. Grill some crusty bread alongside (you'll find it goes with everything) and serve with creamy burrata cheese; mix up a pitcher of sangria or a frosty lime shandy, and your friends may never leave. When you have more time to plan, you can brine wings in honey and salt, toss shrimp with a Vietnamese-style sauce, and dollop oysters with an herbed shallot butter (and serve with a basil-infused gin cocktail). But even these hors d'oeuvres aren't fussy at all. They're just incredibly delicious, and they elevate the notion of what an appetizer can be.

Honey-Brined Chicken Wings

SERVES 6 TO 8

Brining—soaking in a solution of salt, water, and sometimes sugar—results in moist, tender meat. The honey rounds out the flavor of this brine and aids in caramelization on the grill. Wings are the ultimate grab-and-go food, made sweet and spicy here with an additional drizzle of chile-flecked honey. Serve them with a refreshing, tall drink, such as our twist on a standard Southern cocktail, Bourbon Mint Tea (page 69).

½ cup coarse salt

¾ cup honey

2½ pounds whole chicken wings and drumettes

Vegetable oil, for grill

1 teaspoon red-pepper flakes

½ teaspoon chile powder, such as ancho

Bring 6 cups water, the salt, and ½ cup honey to a simmer in a medium saucepan over medium-low heat, stirring until salt dissolves. Let cool completely.

Place chicken in a large bowl and pour cooled brine over top. Refrigerate, covered, at least 2 hours and up to 24 hours. Remove meat from brine, rinse under cold water, and pat dry with paper towels.

Heat grill to medium. Lightly oil grates. Grill chicken, turning often, until cooked through, about 15 minutes.

Meanwhile, combine remaining ¼ cup honey, the red-pepper flakes, and chile powder. Serve chicken drizzled with chile honey.

Kielbasa Bites with Potato Salad

SERVES 12

Smoked Polish pork sausage is a quick starter on the grill, since kielbasa has already been cured—all you have to do is heat the sausage until you see pleasing grill marks. Slicing the kielbasa lengthwise before cooking means that more surface area is in contact with the grill, for better charring. It contrasts nicely with buttery Yukon Gold potatoes coated in a light grainy-mustard vinaigrette, which you can make up to two days in advance. Serve with your favorite sauerkraut.

1 **pound baby Yukon Gold or new potatoes, peeled and sliced ½ inch thick**

Coarse salt and freshly ground pepper

¼ **cup vegetable oil, plus more for grill**

2 **tablespoons white-wine vinegar**

1 **tablespoon plus 1 teaspoon grainy mustard**

3 **tablespoons snipped fresh chives**

2 **pounds kielbasa, halved lengthwise**

Sauerkraut, for serving

Cover potatoes by 2 inches of water in a medium saucepan; add 1 tablespoon salt. Bring to a boil, reduce to a simmer, and cook until just tender, 10 to 15 minutes. Drain and return to hot saucepan to dry, 5 minutes. Immediately toss with oil, vinegar, mustard, and 1½ teaspoons salt; season with pepper. Refrigerate until cool, at least 30 minutes and up to 2 days. Stir in chives.

Heat grill to high. Lightly oil grates. Grill kielbasa until heated through and charred, about 3 minutes per side. Transfer to a cutting board and cut crosswise on the bias into 2-inch pieces. Serve with potato salad and sauerkraut.

Italian Sausages and Tomatoes on Focaccia

SERVES 4 TO 6

This play on a deconstructed sausage pizza makes for a much in-demand appetizer. Slices of focaccia are first spread with a fresh relish of grilled tomatoes, oregano, salt, and pepper, then topped with halved links. You can substitute ciabatta or rustic Italian bread for the focaccia.

4 tomatoes (about 2¼ pounds), halved crosswise

Coarse salt and freshly ground pepper

2 tablespoons extra-virgin olive oil, plus more for grill and drizzling

¼ cup fresh oregano leaves, coarsely chopped

6 sweet or spicy Italian sausages

6 slices focaccia, each approximately 6 by 4 inches

Heat grill to medium-high. Season tomatoes with salt and pepper, and drizzle with oil. Lightly oil grates. Grill tomatoes, cut-side down, until charred in spots and beginning to soften, 5 to 7 minutes. Turn tomatoes, and grill until soft and juicy but still holding their shape, 5 to 7 minutes more. Transfer to a cutting board; let cool slightly. Coarsely chop, then transfer to a medium bowl. Add oregano and toss to combine. Season with salt and pepper, and stir in 2 tablespoons oil.

Grill sausages, turning occasionally, until browned and cooked through, about 12 minutes. Cut each sausage in half lengthwise. Using a slotted spoon, divide tomato relish among focaccia. Top each with 2 sausage halves and fold to eat.

Kofta Kebabs

MAKES 18 SKEWERS

The seasoned ground meat known as *kofta* has many variations; while lamb or beef is typically used, we also think ground dark-meat turkey holds its own. Kofta is usually served with a cooling yogurt sauce; ours includes *za'atar,* a Middle Eastern spice blend of sesame seeds, sumac, and dried herbs such as thyme and marjoram. Garlic-forward Lebanese Tomato Sauce and Chopped-Chile Relish offer a touch of heat in counterpoint. Serve the kebabs with pita bread, sliced cucumbers, tomatoes, red onion, and fresh mint.

2 **pounds ground lamb or dark-meat turkey**

1 **medium onion, finely chopped**

1 **cup finely chopped fresh flat-leaf parsley leaves**

2 **tablespoons extra-virgin olive oil, plus more for grill**

2 **teaspoons cumin seeds, toasted and ground**

¾ **teaspoon ground cinnamon**

Coarse salt and freshly ground pepper

Yogurt-Cucumber Sauce (page 239)

Lebanese Tomato Sauce (page 239)

Chopped-Chile Relish (page 239)

Soak 18 wooden skewers, if using, in water 30 minutes.

In a large bowl, gently stir together meat, onion, parsley, oil, cumin, cinnamon, 1½ teaspoons salt (or 2½ teaspoons, if using ground turkey), and ½ teaspoon pepper until just combined (do not overmix). Using your hands, form ¼ cup of meat mixture into a 3-inch-long oval and place on a rimmed baking sheet brushed with oil. Repeat with remaining mixture. Refrigerate, covered, at least 1 hour and up to 24 hours.

Heat grill to medium-high. Thread each meat oval onto a skewer. Lightly oil grates. Grill kebabs, turning as needed, until cooked through and charred in spots, and an instant-read thermometer inserted in each middle (avoiding skewers) registers 160°F (for medium) for lamb, 6 to 8 minutes; or 165°F for turkey, 10 to 12 minutes. Serve with Yogurt-Cucumber Sauce, Lebanese Tomato Sauce, and Chopped Chile Relish.

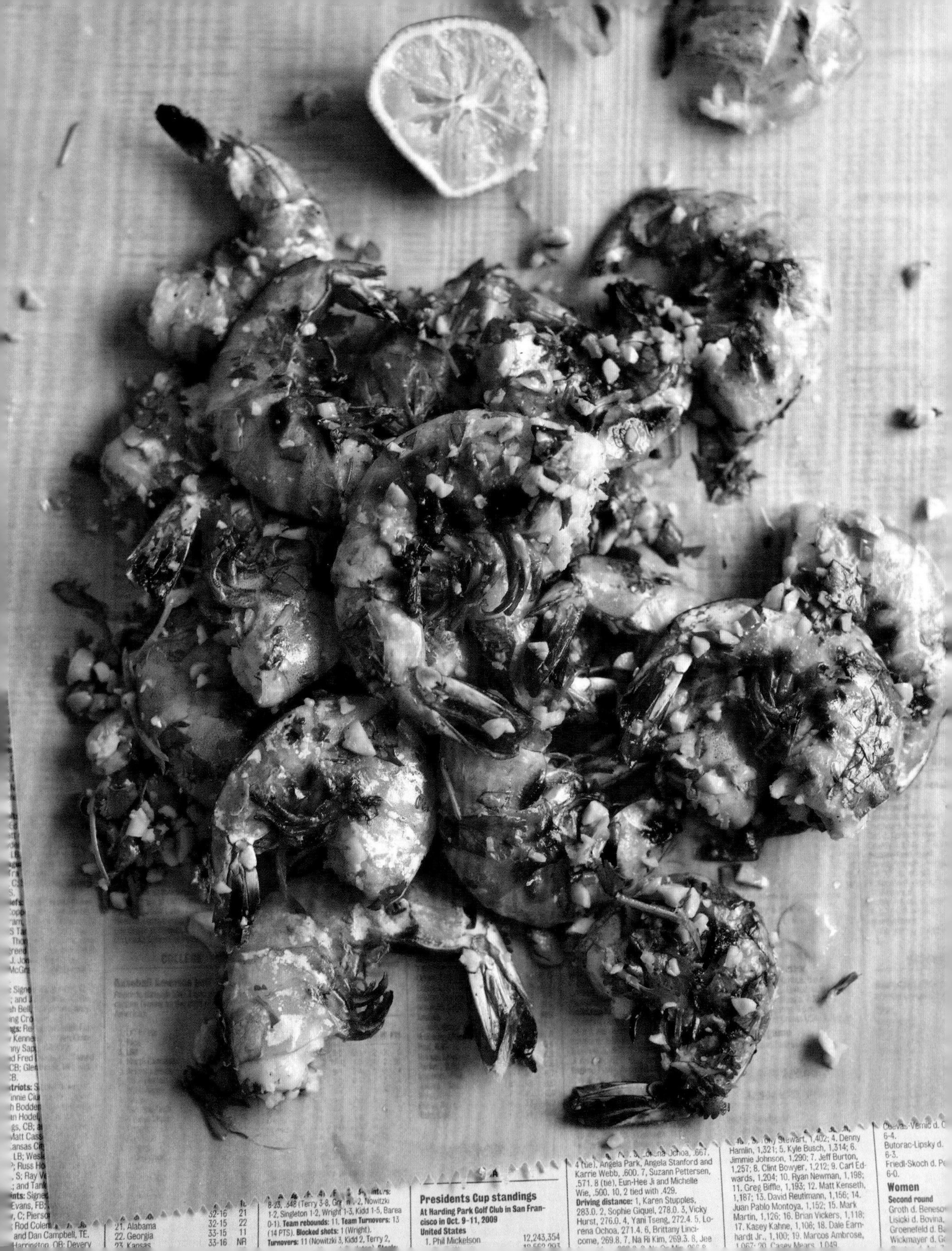

Presidents Cup standings

Shrimp with Cilantro, Lime, and Peanuts

SERVES 4

Before tossing the shrimp in this vibrantly flavored Vietnamese-style sauce, grill them with the shells on to seal in the flavor. Shrimp should be deveined before cooking: Use a sharp paring knife to make a slit along the back of each shrimp, and with the tip of the knife, pull up on the vein to remove it.

2 limes

2 teaspoons fish sauce

½ teaspoon sugar

2 teaspoons vegetable oil, plus more for grill

1 pound jumbo shrimp (about 15), shells on, deveined

Coarse salt and freshly ground pepper

1½ cups coarsely chopped fresh cilantro

½ cup roasted salted peanuts, coarsely chopped

2 scallions, finely chopped

Using a microplane zester, finely grate zest of limes into a small bowl. Squeeze in juice from 1 lime. Whisk in fish sauce and sugar.

Heat grill to high. Lightly oil grates. Brush shrimp with oil on both sides; lightly season with salt and pepper. Grill until pink and firm to the touch, 2 to 3 minutes per side.

Toss shrimp with fish-sauce mixture, cilantro, peanuts, and scallions until thoroughly coated. Squeeze juice from remaining lime over shrimp and serve immediately.

Grilled Oysters with Fennel-Shallot Butter

SERVES 4

The intense heat of the grill is ideal for direct-cooking oysters. As the oysters cook, their shells will pop open slightly; you'll need a knife to open them completely. Be sure to hold them with the curved shells down, which will catch the saline liquor when the flat top shells are removed. Fennel fronds add a delicate, aromatic accent to this shallot butter; but finely grated lemon zest makes a nice substitute. You can further enhance the anise flavor with a few drops of an aperitif, such as Pernod or absinthe, stirred into the butter. To accompany the oysters, serve an effervescent Basil French 75 cocktail (page 69).

1 tablespoon finely chopped fennel fronds

1 small shallot, finely chopped

½ cup (1 stick) unsalted butter, room temperature

Coarse salt and freshly ground pepper

12 oysters

Heat grill to high. Stir fennel fronds and shallot thoroughly into butter, and season with salt and pepper. Refrigerate until ready to use or up to overnight. Place oysters directly on grill, with curved side of their shells down.

Grill until oysters begin to open, 2 to 5 minutes (depending on size). Remove each oyster from grill as soon as it opens up. Transfer oysters to a platter, curved-side down, returning any that did not open to grill (if, after 5 to 10 minutes, they have not opened, discard them). Holding each oyster with a kitchen towel, use an oyster knife to open further, keeping curved side down. Spoon a small amount of fennel-shallot butter on top of each one and serve immediately.

TIP: Keep the oysters on ice until you're ready to grill. Once they're cooked, you'll need to be ready to serve and eat, so pour your drinks first and gather your supplies—two thick kitchen towels, grill tongs, an oyster knife, and a platter to hold the hot oysters.

Grilled Fresh Sardines with Crostini

SERVES 4

Sardines don't require a lot of dressing up, since their bold flavor speaks for itself. We like to prepare them as they are enjoyed in the Mediterranean region—tossed in olive oil and grilled to perfection. Serve them just as simply—with garlicky grilled bread and fresh lemons.

8 whole fresh sardines (about 1 pound total), cleaned, rinsed inside and out, and patted dry

Extra-virgin olive oil, for grill and brushing

Coarse salt and freshly ground pepper

1 (6-inch) baguette piece, cut on the diagonal into thin slices

1 garlic clove, halved

Lemon wedges, for serving

Heat grill to medium-high. Brush both sides of sardines with oil. Season with ½ teaspoon salt.

Rub bread with cut sides of garlic. Brush with oil, and sprinkle with salt and pepper.

Lightly oil grates. Grill bread, turning once, until golden brown and lightly charred, less than 1 minute per side. Grill sardines, turning once, until cooked through and well charred, about 2 minutes per side. Sprinkle with salt, and serve with crostini and lemon wedges.

Shishito Peppers and Chorizo

MAKES 12 SKEWERS

These Japanese chiles, which are in the same family as the padrón pepper, are slightly sweet and take on a delicious smoky flavor when charred. They range in color from light green to a mature red, with the latter tasting meatier and a bit spicier than the milder light green. Here, we grill the peppers with Spanish chorizo, but they also fly solo beautifully, with just a sprinkle of salt.

24 **shishito peppers**

24 **one-inch pieces (1 pound) dried chorizo**

Vegetable oil, for grill

Coarse salt

Soak 12 wooden skewers, if using, in water 30 minutes.

Thread 2 peppers and 2 chorizo pieces onto each skewer. Meanwhile, heat grill to medium-high. Lightly oil grates. Grill, turning often, until peppers are blistered and chorizo shows char marks, about 3 minutes. Sprinkle with salt and serve immediately.

Red-Curry Salmon Bites

MAKES 14 SKEWERS

Salmon is a wonderful fish to cook on the grill, as it's less delicate than other varieties, such as sole. Here, we've prepared it using fillet strips on skewers, keeping the skin on to help the fish stay intact. This appetizer is endlessly customizable—we added instant heat with curry paste, but you can add oil to your favorite spice rub and brush it on the salmon; or make a paste from Madras curry powder, minced shallot, lime zest, a pinch of sugar, and oil. Be sure to grill the fish just until it's done, as it will begin to flake off the skewers if overcooked.

1 **skin-on salmon fillet (about 1¼ pounds; no more than 1 inch thick; preferably tail end)**

2 **tablespoons Thai red-curry paste**

2 **tablespoons vegetable oil, plus more for grill**

Lime wedges, for serving

Soak 14 wooden skewers, if using, in water 30 minutes.

Using a sharp knife, slice salmon fillet into strips about 1 inch wide and 3 inches long. In a medium bowl, stir together curry paste and oil; add salmon and coat on all sides. (If not cooking immediately, salmon can be refrigerated, covered, up to 8 hours.) Thread salmon strips lengthwise onto skewers.

Heat grill to medium-high. Lightly oil grates. Sear salmon until strips can be lifted with a metal spatula, 1 to 2 minutes. Turn and cook until flesh is just opaque but before it flakes when pressed, 1 to 1½ minutes. Serve on skewers, with lime wedges on the side for squeezing.

Charred Okra with Paprika and Fresh Thyme

MAKES 30 SKEWERS

Cooking okra quickly over high heat helps keep the Southern favorite crisp-tender. For easy grilling, thread the vegetable from stem to tip on a skewer. We serve it with thyme and hot paprika for a Creole-inspired snack.

1 pound okra (about 30 pieces)

Extra-virgin olive oil, for brushing and grill

2 teaspoons fresh thyme leaves

1½ teaspoons hot paprika

1 tablespoon flaky sea salt, such as Maldon

Soak 30 wooden skewers, if using, in water 30 minutes.

Heat grill to high. Thread each okra from stem to tip onto skewers and brush with oil. Combine thyme, paprika, and salt in a small bowl.

Lightly oil grates. Grill okra, turning a few times until charred in places and crisp-tender, about 4 minutes total. Remove from grill and sprinkle with thyme mixture.

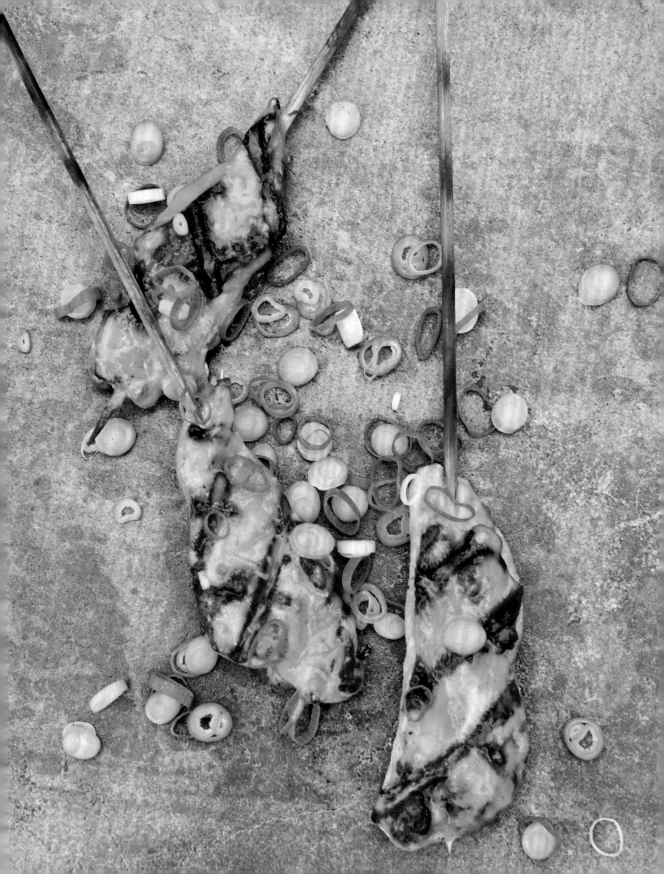

Chicken Satay

MAKES 12 SKEWERS

The Southeast Asian method of marinating chicken, grilling the tender meat, and then serving it with a smooth peanut sauce has made satay a classic crowd-pleaser. Sliced into bite-size pieces, the chicken cooks in less than 5 minutes.

2 boneless, skinless chicken breast halves (6 to 8 ounces each), thinly sliced lengthwise into 12 strips

1 teaspoon toasted sesame oil

1 teaspoon soy sauce

1 garlic clove, minced

Coarse salt

½ teaspoon red-pepper flakes, or to taste

¼ cup creamy peanut butter

2 tablespoons unseasoned rice vinegar

Vegetable oil, for grill

Thinly sliced scallions, for serving

Soak 12 wooden skewers, if using, in water 30 minutes.

Toss chicken with sesame oil, soy sauce, garlic, ½ teaspoon salt, and ¼ teaspoon red-pepper flakes in a medium bowl. (If not cooking immediately, chicken can be refrigerated, covered, up to 8 hours.) Thread each chicken strip lengthwise onto a skewer.

Whisk together peanut butter, vinegar, and remaining ¼ teaspoon red-pepper flakes in a small bowl. Whisk in up to 3 tablespoons water, 1 tablespoon at a time, until mixture reaches desired consistency.

Heat grill to high. Lightly oil grates. Working in batches, cook chicken until opaque and cooked through, 1 to 2 minutes per side. Sprinkle chicken with scallions and serve with dipping sauce.

Grilled Spring Vegetables with Almond Aïoli and Anchoïade

SERVES 6

A study in brilliant green comes with four of spring's freshest flavors, served with rustic Provençal sauces. Asparagus and spring onions are familiar with the grill, but fava beans and garlic scapes are a delicious surprise. Grill and eat the favas, pods and all, which saves you from the finicky shelling usually required. Do make sure to choose very young beans—the pods are much more tender. Scapes, the pungent, chewy tops of the hardneck garlic plant, take on a mild, sweet flavor when lightly charred.

4 to 6 spring onions

1 bunch asparagus (about 1 pound), trimmed

1 pound fava beans in the pod

4 to 6 garlic scapes

Extra-virgin olive oil, for drizzling and grill

Coarse salt

Almond aïoli (page 242), for serving

Anchoïade (page 242), for serving

Heat grill to medium-high, with an indirect-heat zone. On a rimmed baking sheet, drizzle spring onions, asparagus, fava beans, and garlic scapes with oil and toss to lightly coat; season with salt.

Lightly oil grates. Grill vegetables directly on grates, turning occasionally. For spring onions, grill until softened and bulb is charred in spots, 5 to 7 minutes; move greens over indirect heat to avoid charring, if necessary. For fava beans, cook, turning once, until softened and charred in spots, about 5 minutes. For asparagus, cook until tender, 2 to 4 minutes, depending on thickness; move over indirect heat to avoid charring, if necessary. For garlic scapes, cook until softened and lightly charred, about 3 minutes.

Serve vegetables warm with sauces.

Grilled Vegetable Antipasto

EACH RECIPE MAKES 4 SKEWERS

For a quick, tasty bite, grill a variety of seasonal vegetables on skewers (soaked in water for 30 minutes, if using wooden). Remove them from the skewers and arrange on a serving platter as you would a classic antipasto: with olives, breadsticks, and cured meats, if desired. Or serve the skewers hot off the grill, with dipping sauces (pages 237 to 242).

Artichoke and Crusty Bread

- 2 cans (15 ounces each) artichoke hearts, drained and patted dry
- ½ loaf crusty bread, torn in large pieces

Eggplant and Bell Pepper

- 1 eggplant, cut into ½-inch pieces
- 1 bell pepper, stemmed, seeded, and ribs removed, cut into ½-inch pieces

  Red-pepper flakes

Scallion and Mushroom

- 5 ounces mixed mushrooms, trimmed
- 4 scallions, cut into 3-inch pieces

Potato, Celery, and Onion

- 8 ounces small potatoes, scrubbed, boiled until just tender, and halved
- 2 celery stalks, sliced crosswise in ½-inch pieces
- 1 medium red onion, cut into 1-inch wedges

  Snipped fresh chives

Tomato and Bocconcini

- 1 pound cocktail tomatoes or large cherry tomatoes
- 4 to 8 bocconcini

  Fresh oregano leaves

  Extra-virgin olive oil, for grill and drizzling

  Coarse salt and freshly ground pepper

For all vegetables, heat grill to medium-high. Thread ingredients onto 4 skewers, in alternating order (if making tomato and bocconcini, only thread tomatoes). Generously drizzle skewered vegetables with oil and season with salt. (Add black pepper, if grilling artichokes or mushrooms.) Lightly oil grates. Grill, turning occasionally, until lightly charred (see chart below for times).

Sprinkle eggplant and bell pepper with red-pepper flakes. Sprinkle potato, celery, and onion with chives. Sprinkle tomato and bocconcini with fresh oregano.

COOK TIMES

Artichoke and Crusty Bread: 2 to 3 minutes

Eggplant and Bell Pepper: 8 to 9 minutes

Scallion and Mushroom: 3 to 5 minutes

Potato, Celery, and Onion: 7 to 8 minutes

Tomato: 4 to 5 minutes (then add 1 to 2 bocconcini on either end of skewer and grill 30 seconds more)

Grilled Bread and Chiles with Burrata Cheese

SERVES 4 TO 6

Take advantage of the many assorted chiles and sweet peppers at the markets in late summer by serving them as simply as can be: grilled with bread and cheese. Balance some of the chiles' heat with a refreshing aperitif, such as an Upside-Down Martini (page 69), which is more spritz than boozy cocktail, subbing in the fresh and slightly effervescent Portuguese vinho verde for the vermouth.

Extra-virgin olive oil, for grill and drizzling

1 **pound mixed peppers and chiles of varied sizes**

8 **thick slices crusty bread**

2 **(4-ounce) balls burrata cheese**

Coarse salt and freshly ground pepper

Heat grill to medium-high. Lightly oil grates. Grill peppers whole, turning occasionally, until skin is mostly blackened and peppers are completely softened, 5 to 10 minutes depending on their size. Place in a medium bowl and cover 10 to 15 minutes. When cool enough to handle, remove skins and pull peppers apart, discarding skins, seeds, and stems, if desired. Tear in half if small, or cut into strips about ¾ inch wide.

Lightly oil both sides of each bread slice and grill, turning once, until marked by the grill and beginning to crisp, 2 to 3 minutes. Divide burrata among plates, drizzle generously with oil, and season with salt and pepper. Serve burrata with grilled bread and peppers.

Grilled Peaches and Figs with Prosciutto and Robiola

SERVES 10

Grilling stone fruits and figs deepens their natural sweetness. Pair them with prosciutto and a soft Italian cheese like Robiola for an unbeatable flavor trifecta: sweet, smoky, and salty. When selecting fruits, make sure it yields gently to the touch but is not too soft. You want it at just the right stage of ripeness so it will hold up over high heat. Serve with an Americano (page 69), a bittersweet and refreshing cocktail.

Extra-virgin olive oil

5 medium peaches, ripe but firm, halved, pits removed

10 fresh figs, halved

Coarse salt and freshly ground pepper

4 ounces thinly sliced prosciutto, for serving

8 ounces Robiola cheese

Breadsticks and crackers, for serving

Heat grill to medium-high. Lightly oil grates. Brush peaches and figs with oil. Season with salt and pepper.

Grill peaches and figs, turning occasionally, until charred and softened, about 2 minutes. Transfer to a platter. Season fruits with pepper and drizzle with oil. Serve with prosciutto, Robiola, and breadsticks and crackers.

Craft Cocktails

EACH MAKES 1 DRINK

There are no firm rules when it comes to matching cocktails with grilled food—just make them delicious, icy cold, and fun. Here's a collection that fits the bill, including a Kentucky Derby–ready spiked tea (shown), an effervescent gin drink, an invigorating martini-alternative, and a barkeeper's bittersweet classic.

Bourbon Mint Tea

- 1 tablespoon sugar
- ½ cup boiling water
- 1 black-tea bag
- 1 tablespoon fresh mint leaves
- 2 ounces (¼ cup) bourbon
  Ice cubes

Combine sugar and boiling water in a pitcher, and stir to dissolve. Add tea bag and steep (discard tea bag). Add ½ cup cold water and refrigerate until chilled. Add mint leaves and muddle until fragrant. Stir in bourbon and serve over ice.

Basil French 75

- 5 basil leaves, plus more for serving
- 1 teaspoon superfine sugar
- 2 ounces (¼ cup) gin
- 1 tablespoon fresh lemon juice
  Ice cubes
- 4 ounces (½ cup) champagne

Muddle basil leaves with sugar in a shaker. Add gin, lemon juice, and ice. Shake and strain into an ice-filled glass. Top with champagne. Serve immediately.

Upside-Down Martini

- ¾ ounce gin
  Ice cubes
- 2 ounces (¼ cup) vinho verde
- 3 pimiento-stuffed green olives

Pour gin over ice in a small glass. Top with vinho verde and stir. Add olives. Serve immediately.

Americano

- 2 ounces (¼ cup) sweet vermouth
- 2 ounces (¼ cup) Campari
- 2 ounces (¼ cup) club soda
  Ice cubes
  Orange slice, for serving

Mix vermouth, Campari, and club soda in a tall glass filled with ice. Garnish with orange slice. Serve immediately.

Beer Cocktails

EACH SERVES 6

There's no denying the allure of hot barbecue and cold beer. But beer doesn't have to be sipped straight up—it can be mixed as well as any spirit (take the spicy michelada, with beer, hot chile sauce, tomato juice, and limes). Our lively shandies use limeade or freshly squeezed lemons instead of the traditional lemonade. And our take on *kriek lambic*, a sweet Belgian beer brewed with cherries, is a pale ale combined with sour-cherry nectar.

Lime Shandy

- 1½ cups fresh lime juice (from about 25 limes), plus wedges for serving
- ½ cup superfine sugar

  Ice cubes
- 2 (12-ounce) bottles Mexican beer or pilsner

  Coarse salt, for serving

Combine lime juice and sugar with 4 cups water in a large pitcher. Stir until sugar is dissolved. Fill another large pitcher with ice. Pour in beer and 1⅓ cups lime-sugar mixture, and stir to combine. Pour into salt-rimmed glasses and serve with lime wedges.

Lemon Shandy

- ⅓ cup superfine sugar
- ½ cup fresh lemon juice (from about 3 lemons), plus wedges, for serving
- 6 (12-ounce) mild pilsner beers

Chill six 16-ounce glasses or mugs. In a small saucepan, combine sugar and ½ cup water over medium heat. Cook, stirring until sugar dissolves, about 1 minute. Refrigerate until cool, at least 10 minutes and up to 1 week.

In a small pitcher, combine sugar mixture and lemon juice. Pour 1 beer into each chilled glass, then add about ¼ cup lemon mixture. Serve with lemon wedges.

Cherry Beer

- Ice cubes
- 2 (12-ounce) bottles pale ale
- 1½ cups sour-cherry nectar, such as Tamek

  Lemon wedges, for serving

Fill a large pitcher with ice. Pour in pale ale and sour-cherry nectar, and stir to combine. Pour into glasses, garnish with lemon wedges, and serve.

Three Sangrias

EACH SERVES 6

Sangria's winning combination of chilled fruit and wine can be dressed up and down in a multitude of ways. Try these variations on the original: use sherry, warm-weather favorite rosé, or white wine and mint, then experiment further—and do plenty of taste-testing.

Sherry Sangria

- 1 bottle (750 milliliters) amontillado sherry
- 1 cup Cointreau or Grand Marnier
- 8 to 10 ounces frozen, pitted red cherries
- 1½ to 2 pounds sliced fresh stone fruit, such as apricots, peaches, and plums

  Ice cubes, for serving

Combine sherry, Cointreau, and fruit in a pitcher. Let stand in refrigerator at least 1 hour or up to overnight. Serve over ice.

Sparkling Rosé Sangria

- 1 tablespoon fresh organic lavender buds (optional)
- 2 teaspoons sugar
- 2 cups strawberries
- 8 green figs, halved
- 2 cups mixed red and golden raspberries
- 3 cups chilled dry rosé wine
- 1 bottle (250 milliliters) chilled sparkling wine, such as cava

  Ice cubes, for serving

Using a mortar and pestle, grind together 2 teaspoons lavender buds, if using, with sugar until fragrant. Toss with strawberries, figs, and raspberries, and allow to macerate at least 30 minutes or up to 4 hours.

Place fruit in a chilled pitcher along with accumulated juices, remaining teaspoon lavender buds, if using, and rosé. Stir well, top with sparkling wine, and serve over ice.

White Sangria

- ½ medium honeydew melon, cut into 1-inch pieces
- ½ medium English cucumber, sliced into thin spears
- 1 lime, thinly sliced crosswise
- 1 cup fresh mint leaves
- ¼ cup elderflower liqueur, such as St-Germain, or syrup
- ½ cup silver tequila
- 1 bottle (750 milliliters) dry white wine

  Ice cubes, for serving

Combine melon, cucumber, lime, mint, elderflower liqueur, and tequila in a large pitcher. Stir to combine. Let stand in refrigerator at least 1 hour or up to overnight. Pour in wine and stir to combine. Serve over ice.

Iced Teas with a Citrus Twist

EACH SERVES 2

Inspired by the pairing that launched the Arnold Palmer—tea with a splash of lemonade—we've crafted three colorful duos. Fresh orange, lime, and grapefruit juices invigorate gentle jasmine, chamomile, and rooibos herbal teas for grillside drinks that are built to refresh.

Jasmine Tea and Orange Juice

- 2 teaspoons loose-leaf or 2 bags jasmine tea
- 2 cups boiling water
- 2 cups fresh orange juice (6 to 8 oranges)
- Ice cubes, for serving
- Orange slices, for serving

Steep tea in boiling water 4 minutes; strain or remove bags. Let cool completely, then combine orange juice and tea in a pitcher. Refrigerate until ready to serve, up to 2 days. Serve over ice, garnished with orange slices.

Chamomile Tea and Limeade

- 2 teaspoons loose-leaf or 2 bags chamomile tea
- 2 cups boiling water
- ½ cup sugar
- Juice of 3 limes (⅓ cup)
- Ice cubes, for serving
- Lime wedges, for serving

Steep tea in boiling water 4 minutes; strain or remove bags. Let cool completely. Meanwhile, combine sugar and ½ cup water in a small saucepan. Bring to a boil, stirring until sugar is dissolved. Let cool completely, then combine with lime juice and tea in a pitcher. Refrigerate until ready to serve, up to 2 days. Serve over ice, garnished with lime wedges.

Rooibos Tea and Grapefruit

- 2 teaspoons loose-leaf or 2 bags rooibos tea
- 2 cups boiling water
- ½ cup sugar
- Juice of 2 Ruby Red grapefruits (1 cup)
- Ice cubes, for serving
- Grapefruit slices, for serving

Steep tea in boiling water 4 minutes; strain or remove bags. Let cool completely. Meanwhile, combine sugar and ½ cup water in a small saucepan. Bring to a boil, stirring until sugar is dissolved. Let cool completely, then combine with grapefruit juice and tea in a pitcher. Let stand in refrigerator until ready to serve, up to 2 days. Serve over ice, garnished with grapefruit slices.

As a Main

In this chapter, we've collected the best of the best—reliable recipes you'll want to master, and turn to again and again. Begin by learning the basics, like how to perfectly grill a whole bird (spatchcocking is the secret). Then familiarize yourself with the finest cuts of meat, and the rubs and brines to go with them: Grill a rib-eye and top with jalapeño butter when it's just two of you; or marinate a leg of lamb with fresh mint, garlic, and lemon for a big group. For chicken, we advise a basic dry brine of salt and pepper, but for an extra-juicy pork chop, opt for a wet brine. Of course, it wouldn't be grilling season without seafood: There's sweet-and-spicy shrimp, a whole fish stuffed with fresh herbs, and even a lobster grilled in its shell, to name just a few. While there are myriad ways to grill a meal, we've selected our favorites—in other words, our signature dishes, soon to be yours.

Buttermilk-and-Rosemary-Brined Chicken

SERVES 12

A soak in herb-laced buttermilk seasons bone-in chicken pieces through and through, while also tenderizing the meat. The key to grilling chicken is to start over indirect heat for low-and-slow cooking to avoid burning, then move to direct heat for a final light char. If you have extra rosemary sprigs and some citrus peel on hand, grill them over direct heat for an aromatic garnish. You can serve this chicken hot or cold (it's great picnic fare) with Potato and Green Bean Salad (page 193) or Peach Panzanella (page 197), and plenty of napkins for messy fingers.

4 **cups buttermilk**

15 **garlic cloves**

1 **cup fresh rosemary or thyme leaves**

 Coarse salt and freshly ground pepper

3 **whole chickens (about 3 pounds each), cut into 10 pieces each**

 Vegetable oil, for grill

Combine buttermilk, garlic, herbs, 2 tablespoons salt, and 2 teaspoons pepper.

Divide chicken between 2 large shallow baking dishes. Pour in marinade, turning to coat. Refrigerate, covered, at least 4 hours or up to overnight, turning chicken occasionally. Let stand at room temperature 30 minutes to 1 hour before grilling.

Heat grill to medium, with an indirect-heat zone. Lightly oil grates. Remove chicken from marinade, letting excess drip off (discard marinade); pat dry with paper towels. Place chicken over indirect heat. Cover and cook, turning occasionally, until pieces are cooked through and an instant-read thermometer inserted into thickest parts registers 165°F, about 30 minutes. Uncover grill and transfer chicken to direct heat. Cook, turning once, until lightly charred, 3 to 4 minutes.

TIP: Letting the chicken come to room temperature and patting it dry before grilling helps it cook more evenly and achieve a good sear; this is good practice for all cuts of meat, and especially helpful with bone-in meats and poultry.

Lemon-Herb Spatchcocked Chicken

SERVES 4

Spatchcocking—also known as butterflying—in which a whole bird is split and flattened, enables you to cook the meat evenly while achieving a super-crisp skin. Your butcher can do this for you, but it's straightforward with a pair of kitchen shears. Spatchcocking makes it possible to pull off a whole chicken on a weeknight, especially when you brine, rub, or marinate the meat the night before. While the grill is hot, add some lemon halves to serve with the chicken.

1 whole chicken (3 to 3½ pounds)

1 medium onion, halved

1 large garlic clove

⅓ cup fresh herbs, such as rosemary, thyme, flat-leaf parsley, and sage

¼ cup extra-virgin olive oil, plus more for grill

Zest of ½ lemon, removed in strips with a peeler

Coarse salt and freshly ground pepper

To spatchcock chicken, cut along each side of the backbone with shears. Remove backbone (it can be stored in the freezer for stock up to 3 months). Turn chicken breast-side up; flatten it by pressing firmly on the upper part with your palm.

Puree onion, garlic, herbs, oil, and zest in a food processor. Rub some onion mixture under skin of chicken breast. Rub remaining onion mixture over rest of bird. Refrigerate, covered, at least 6 hours or up to overnight. Let stand at room temperature 30 minutes to 1 hour. Wipe off most of rub; season with salt and pepper.

Heat grill to medium-high, with an indirect-heat zone. Lightly oil grates. Place chicken over indirect heat, breast-side down. Cover and cook until an instant-read thermometer inserted into thickest part of thigh and breast (avoiding bone) registers 165°F, about 30 minutes. Uncover grill and transfer chicken to direct heat. Cook, turning once, until skin is crisp and lightly charred, 3 to 4 minutes. Let stand 10 minutes before serving.

TIP: If your grill is big enough, double the recipe and serve leftovers cold over salad.

Chicken with Green Chile Dressing

SERVES 4

The techniques of dry-brining chicken before grilling and later brushing it with a post-grill dressing come in handy when you don't have time to let your chicken marinate for hours. This all-purpose salt-and-pepper rub keeps meat moist and tender while it cooks, and the post-grill dressing, here a riff on salsa verde, preserves the bright, fresh flavors of the herbs.

Coarse salt and freshly ground pepper

1 whole chicken (about 4 pounds), cut into 10 pieces (breasts halved)

1 cup fresh cilantro leaves, coarsely chopped

1 serrano chile, seeded and chopped

2 scallions, chopped

Zest of 1 lime plus 2 tablespoons fresh juice

¼ cup extra-virgin olive oil, plus more for grill and brushing

Combine 1 tablespoon salt and ½ teaspoon pepper, and sprinkle evenly over chicken. Set chicken on a rimmed baking sheet and refrigerate 1 hour or up to overnight (bring to room temperature before grilling).

For dressing, combine cilantro, chile, scallions, lime zest and juice, and oil. Season with salt.

Heat grill to medium, with an indirect-heat zone. Lightly oil grates. Lightly brush chicken with oil and place over indirect heat. Cover and cook, turning occasionally, until pieces are cooked through and an instant-read thermometer inserted into thickest parts (avoiding bone) registers 165°F, about 30 minutes. Uncover grill and transfer chicken to direct heat. Cook, turning once, until lightly charred, 3 to 4 minutes. Brush dressing over chicken as it comes off the grill and plate to serve.

Chicken and Vegetable Kebabs

SERVES 4

Sweet, plump cipollini onions caramelize nicely because of their high sugar content, which makes them wonderful for grilling and roasting. They're also a good match for mild zucchini and flavorful cremini mushrooms. Chicken thighs are a smart choice for kebabs, as they stay tender and juicy even when cut into bite-size pieces. Thread each ingredient on its own skewer to ensure uniform cooking. Serve with couscous and Tahini Sauce or Chopped-Chile Relish (pages 237 and 239).

5 boneless, skinless chicken thighs (about 1½ pounds), cut into 1½-inch-wide strips

Coarse salt and freshly ground pepper

3 tablespoons extra-virgin olive oil, plus more for grill and dressing

2 medium zucchini, cut into 1-inch-thick rounds

16 medium cipollini onions (about 10 ounces)

16 medium cremini mushrooms (about 8 ounces), trimmed

Zest and juice of 1 lemon

½ cup coarsely chopped fresh flat-leaf parsley leaves

Soak 10 wooden skewers, if using, in water 30 minutes.

Heat grill to medium-high. Season chicken with salt and pepper; toss with 1 tablespoon oil. Season vegetables with salt and pepper; toss with remaining 2 tablespoons oil. Thread chicken onto 4 skewers. Thread vegetables separately onto remaining skewers.

Lightly oil grates. Place onion skewers on grill and cook 5 minutes; turn skewers, and add chicken and zucchini to grill. Cook, turning occasionally, 5 minutes. Add mushroom skewers, and cook, turning occasionally, until chicken is cooked through and vegetables are charred in places, about 10 minutes. Transfer to a plate, and dress with lemon zest and juice, a drizzle of oil, and parsley.

TIP: Kebabs can be assembled and refrigerated up to 3 hours ahead. Let stand at room temperature 30 minutes before grilling.

Peppercorn-Brined Pork Chops

SERVES 4

Brining boosts the juiciness of a lean meat like pork chops.
It's best to use bone-in center-cut rib chops, if you can—they have just
the right amount of fat to stand up to the heat without drying out.
For chicken, we found a simple dry brine works nicely, but with pork,
this wet brine is a winner. Turn the meat frequently for even
cooking without too much char.

½ cup sugar

½ cup coarse salt, plus more for seasoning

4 cups ice cubes

1 fresh bay leaf

1 small bunch fresh thyme, plus sprigs for serving

2 lemons, zest of one removed in strips with a peeler, second one cut into wedges for serving

12 black peppercorns

4 bone-in pork chops, each about 10 ounces and 1 inch thick

Freshly ground pepper

Vegetable oil, for grill and brushing

Bring 4 cups water, the sugar, and salt to a simmer in a large pot, stirring to dissolve. Remove from heat. Add ice, bay leaf, thyme, lemon zest, and peppercorns; let cool completely. Place pork in a large shallow baking dish or resealable plastic bag and cover with brine. Refrigerate, covered, at least 6 hours or up to overnight. Remove pork from brine, letting excess drip off (discard brine); pat dry with paper towels. Let stand at room temperature 30 minutes. Season lightly with salt and pepper.

Heat grill to medium-high. Lightly oil grates. Lightly brush pork with oil and grill, turning as needed, until an instant-read thermometer inserted into thickest parts (avoiding bone) registers 138°F to 145°F for medium, 5 to 7 minutes per side. Transfer pork to a cutting board and let stand 15 minutes. Serve with lemon wedges and thyme.

Pork and Chorizo Kebabs

SERVES 4

Simultaneously grilling two types of pork—loin and chorizo sausage—works magic: As the chorizo cooks, the drippings infuse the pork loin with their spicy, smoky flavor. This recipe makes dinner for four—served with rice or couscous and grilled vegetables—but you can also portion the ingredients among smaller skewers and serve as tapas with Rouille or Romesco (pages 238 and 241) for dipping.

2 boneless pork loin chops, cut into 1½-inch pieces

1 small onion, quartered, layers separated

2 tablespoons extra-virgin olive oil, plus more for grill

1 tablespoon red-wine vinegar

4 ounces dried chorizo sausage, halved lengthwise and cut into ½-inch pieces

Coarse salt and freshly ground pepper

Soak 4 wooden skewers, if using, in water 30 minutes.

Toss pork loin, onion, oil, and vinegar in a large bowl. Cover and marinate at least 1 hour or refrigerate up to overnight (bring to room temperature before grilling).

Heat grill to medium. Beginning and ending with pork loin, thread pork, onion, and chorizo onto skewers. Season with salt and pepper. Lightly oil grates. Grill kebabs, covered, turning occasionally, until pork is cooked through, about 12 minutes.

Lamb Shoulder Chops with Herb Aïoli

SERVES 4

We upgraded our favorite aïoli with a handful of fragrant herbs.
The result is a creamy, aromatic sauce—an impeccable accompaniment
for grilled lamb chops. Shoulder chops are inexpensive cuts, rich in
flavor and just terrific on the grill. Buy them thick (about 1 inch or more)
and cook them over medium-high, turning frequently to allow the fat
to render properly while watching for flare-ups.

½ cup Aïoli (page 241)

2 tablespoons snipped fresh chives

1 tablespoon coarsely chopped fresh
flat-leaf parsley leaves

1½ teaspoons coarsely chopped fresh
rosemary

Coarse salt and freshly ground pepper

4 bone-in lamb shoulder chops, about
1 inch thick

Vegetable oil, for grill

Lemon wedges, for serving

Place aïoli and herbs in a food processor,
and pulse to combine. Season with salt and
pepper. Transfer to a bowl, press plastic
wrap on surface, and refrigerate until ready
to grill, up to 8 hours.

Heat grill to medium-high. Season lamb
with salt and pepper. Lightly oil grates. Grill
lamb, turning often and moving as needed
to avoid flare-ups, about 10 minutes for
medium. Let stand 5 minutes. Serve with
herb aïoli and lemon wedges.

Leg of Lamb with Garlic and Mint

SERVES 12

Grilled leg of lamb is elegant for a special occasion, but easy enough
to make any night of the week. And it doesn't take much to enhance
its inherent flavor. We took our cues from Mediterranean cuisine, and
seasoned it with fresh mint, garlic, and lemon. For this recipe, the lamb
is butterflied and pounded for quick and even cooking, then marinated
overnight. Grilled eggplant and zucchini make ideal partners, along
with pitas, sliced cucumbers, and tapenade (page 237).

1½ cups extra-virgin olive oil, plus more
for grill

1 bunch fresh mint, coarsely chopped;
reserve some leaves for serving

10 to 12 garlic cloves, crushed

Zest of 2 lemons, plus wedges for
serving

Coarse salt and freshly ground black
pepper

½ teaspoon red-pepper flakes

3 pounds boneless leg of lamb (about
half of 1 large leg), butterflied

Combine oil, mint, garlic, zest,
3 tablespoons salt, and red-pepper flakes;
season with black pepper. Reserve ½ cup
marinade, cover, and refrigerate.

Pound lamb to an even 1- to 1½-inch
thickness. Place lamb in a large shallow
baking dish or resealable plastic bag, and
massage marinade into meat. Refrigerate,
covered, overnight.

Let lamb stand at room temperature
1 hour. Heat grill to medium-high. Lightly
oil grates. Remove lamb from marinade,
letting excess drip off (discard marinade);
pat dry with paper towels. Grill lamb,
turning occasionally, until an instant-read
thermometer registers 140°F for medium,
about 20 minutes. Let stand 10 minutes.
Thinly slice lamb against the grain. Drizzle
with reserved marinade and serve with
lemon wedges and mint.

Rib-Eye with Jalapeño Butter

SERVES 2

The secret to a great steak is twofold: First, allow the meat to come to room temperature (never grill a cold steak). Second, season generously—use more salt and pepper than you might think you need. To dress up our rib-eye, we made a compound butter. Here, we use a jalapeño, but you can also stir chopped herbs, garlic, or other ingredients into the softened butter until combined. Leftover compound butter can be refrigerated and used on grilled chops or fish.

½ cup (1 stick) unsalted butter, room temperature

1 jalapeño, seeded and finely chopped

1 garlic clove, minced

1 bone-in rib-eye steak (about 1½ pounds and 1½ inches thick), room temperature

Coarse salt and freshly ground pepper

Vegetable oil, for grill

Flaky sea salt, such as Maldon

Peppery greens, such as Upland Cress or arugula, and thinly sliced onions, for serving

Stir together butter, jalapeño, and garlic in a small bowl.

Heat grill to medium-high, with an indirect-heat zone. Generously season both sides of steak with salt and pepper. Lightly oil grates. Grill steak over direct heat until browned, 3 to 4 minutes per side. Move to indirect heat, and grill, covered, turning once, until an instant-read thermometer registers 125°F to 130°F for medium-rare (avoiding bone), 7 to 8 minutes more per side. Let stand 10 to 15 minutes. Spread about 2 tablespoons jalapeño butter on steak and sprinkle with flaky sea salt. Serve with greens, onion slices, and more jalapeño butter on the side.

Balsamic-Marinated Hanger Steak

SERVES 4 TO 6

Along with flank steak, hanger has big flavor at a lower price point than a high-end cut. It just takes a few hours of marinating to get it ready for the grill. A basic marinade like this one has three components: an acid, an oil, and seasonings. We chose balsamic vinegar for its mellow sweetness, and fresh garlic and plenty of cracked black pepper for a kick. For an unbeatable combination, serve with Sardinian Tomato Salad (page 206).

¼ **cup vegetable oil, plus more for grill**

¼ **cup balsamic vinegar**

1 **tablespoon minced garlic**

Coarse salt and freshly ground pepper

1 **hanger steak (1½ to 2 pounds), cut crosswise into 2 strips and membrane removed**

Combine oil, vinegar, garlic, and 2 teaspoons pepper in a large shallow dish. Add steak, turning to coat. Refrigerate, covered, at least 6 hours or up to overnight. Remove steak from marinade, letting excess drip off (discard marinade); pat dry with paper towels. Let stand at room temperature 30 minutes. Season generously with salt.

Heat grill to medium-high. Lightly oil grates. Grill steak, turning frequently, until an instant-read thermometer registers 125°F to 130°F for medium-rare, about 12 minutes. Transfer steak to a cutting board and let stand at least 5 minutes. Slice steak against the grain before serving.

TIP: To check doneness, insert a thermometer through the steak's side and into the middle, not from the top down (see page 26).

Sirloin and Vegetable Kebabs

SERVES 4

Sirloin tip is a wonderfully versatile and inexpensive cut to cook outdoors—a short time in a marinade makes it juicy when grilled. Drizzle chimichurri—a classic Argentinian sidekick for steaks— over the charred meat and vegetables.

2 tablespoons balsamic vinegar

1 tablespoon soy sauce

Freshly ground pepper

1 pound sirloin tip, cut into 1½-inch pieces

1 medium zucchini, cut into ½-inch rounds

1 small yellow summer squash, cut into ½-inch rounds

1 medium onion, cut into wedges

1 red bell pepper, stemmed, seeded, and ribs removed, cut into 1-inch pieces

Vegetable oil, for grill and brushing

Chimichurri (page 238)

Soak 4 wooden skewers, if using, in water 30 minutes.

Combine vinegar, soy sauce, and ¼ teaspoon pepper in a shallow dish. Add beef and turn to coat. Cover and marinate 30 minutes. Remove beef from marinade, letting excess drip off (discard marinade); pat dry with paper towels.

Heat grill to medium-high. Thread beef onto skewers, alternating with vegetables and brush lightly with oil. Lightly oil grates. Grill kebabs until vegetables are lightly charred and tender, and beef is medium-rare, 7 to 8 minutes per side. Serve kebabs drizzled with chimichurri.

Salmon Fillets with Orange-Herb Butter

SERVES 4

Salmon is transformed with this cayenne-infused citrus butter. It takes just a few minutes over direct heat to produce a truly flavorful crust and tender center. Remember to dab the butter on the fish as it comes off the heat, so it can melt right into the flesh. Serve with some fresh greens or Grilled Corn, Mint, and Scallion Salad (page 198).

½ cup (1 stick) unsalted butter, room temperature

½ teaspoon orange zest plus 2 teaspoons fresh juice

¼ teaspoon cayenne pepper

1 garlic clove, minced

2 tablespoons chopped fresh cilantro

Coarse salt and freshly ground black pepper

4 skin-on salmon fillets (each about 6 ounces)

Vegetable oil, for grill and brushing

Use a fork to mash together butter, orange zest and juice, cayenne, garlic, cilantro, and ½ teaspoon salt.

Heat grill to medium-high. Brush both sides of fish with oil, and season with salt and black pepper. Lightly oil grates. Grill fish, skin-side down, until lightly charred, about 3 minutes. Turn and cook until just opaque in center, about 3 minutes more. Immediately top with orange-herb butter and serve.

Swordfish with Sicilian Oregano–Caper Sauce

SERVES 4

The hearty, meaty nature of a swordfish steak makes it ideal for grilling. Its mildly sweet flavor is complemented here by a lively herbed sauce that also pairs well with other grilled oily fish, such as tuna or mackerel. Serve this with a grain salad, such as Farro with Zucchini, Pine Nuts, and Lemon Zest (page 205).

1 large garlic clove, minced

2 tablespoons fresh lemon juice, plus wedges for serving

1 teaspoon red-wine vinegar

1 tablespoon capers, preferably salt-packed, drained, rinsed, and coarsely chopped

1 tablespoon dried oregano, preferably Sicilian

1 small pepperoncini, coarsely chopped

1 tablespoon chopped fresh thyme leaves

1 tablespoon chopped fresh mint leaves

¼ cup extra-virgin olive oil, plus more for grill

Coarse salt and freshly ground pepper

4 swordfish steaks (each 8 ounces and 1 inch thick)

Stir together garlic, lemon juice, vinegar, capers, oregano, and pepperoncini in a small bowl. Let stand at least 10 minutes and up to 2 hours.

Just before serving, add thyme and mint and stir to combine. Gradually add oil, stirring to combine; season with salt.

Heat grill to medium. Lightly oil grates. Season fish with salt and pepper. Grill fish until marked, then turn and cook, 2 to 4 minutes more for medium-rare. Transfer fish to plates, top with oregano-caper sauce, and serve with lemon wedges.

Sweet and Spicy Grilled Shrimp

SERVES 12

This sweet and fiery sauce gets heat from *sambal oelek*—an Indonesian sauce made with crushed chiles—and tang from lime zest. Brushing it onto the shrimp in a few layers as they grill gives it time to caramelize. Feel free to use other Asian chili sauces; just make sure to taste first to gauge the levels of salt, acidity, and spiciness. Serve with a crunchy side, such as Cabbage and Radish Slaw with Peanut Dressing (page 200).

½ cup sugar

1 teaspoon lime zest plus juice of 3 to 4 limes (about ¼ cup)

1 tablespoon chili paste, such as sambal oelek

1 tablespoon fish sauce

Coarse salt

3 pounds large shrimp (about 36), peeled and deveined (tails left on, optional)

Vegetable oil, for grill

Soak 12 wooden skewers, if using, in water 30 minutes.

Bring sugar and lime juice to a simmer in a small saucepan. Cook, stirring, until sugar dissolves, about 2 minutes. Remove from heat; stir in lime zest, chili paste, and fish sauce.

Heat grill to high. Thread shrimp onto skewers and season with salt. Divide sauce in half and reserve half for serving. Lightly oil grates. Grill shrimp 1 minute and brush with sauce. Turn and grill 1 minute more, and brush with sauce again. Continue to grill, brushing occasionally with sauce, until shrimp is opaque, 1 to 3 minutes more. Serve with reserved sauce.

Grilled Whole Fish with Two Herb Fillings

SERVES 2 TO 4

Cooking whole fish, as opposed to fillets, optimizes flavor and texture because the skin and a thin layer of (healthy) fat insulate the meat. Branzino seems tailor-made for this method: Usually small to medium in size, with white, flaky flesh, and having relatively few bones, it is very easy to serve and eat. We suggest two different citrus and herb fillings—serve them both or choose your favorite.

FOR THE FISH

- 2 whole branzino (each 1 to 1½ pounds), cleaned, heads and tails left intact
- ¼ cup plus 2 tablespoons extra-virgin olive oil, plus more for grill

  Coarse salt and freshly ground pepper

FOR THE DILL-AND-LEMON FILLING

- 1 lemon, half thinly sliced, half cut into wedges
- 3 sprigs dill, plus more for serving

FOR THE BASIL, LIME, AND CHILE FILLING

- 1 lime, half thinly sliced, half cut into wedges
- 3 sprigs basil, plus more for serving
- 3 Thai or serrano chiles, left intact but split down 1 side

Heat grill to medium-high. Drizzle cavity of each fish with 1 tablespoon oil, and season generously with salt and pepper. Stuff one fish cavity with lemon slices and dill, and the other with lime slices, basil, and Thai chiles. (If using just one filling, double ingredient quantities.)

Fasten each cavity opening with a wooden skewer or toothpicks. Using a paring knife, make long, ¼-inch-deep diagonal slashes at 2-inch intervals on both sides of fish. Rub both sides of each fish with remaining ¼ cup oil and season with salt and pepper, working into slashes.

Lightly oil grates. Grill fish, without moving them, until undersides are charred and flesh along slashes turns opaque, 5 to 7 minutes. Using two large metal spatulas, turn fish. (If fish sticks, wait a few seconds until skin sears enough to release cleanly.) Grill until skin is charred and fish are just cooked through and opaque, 5 to 7 minutes more. Serve fish with citrus wedges and herbs.

Grilled Lobster with Mixed Herb Sauce

SERVES 6

Grilled lobster boasts an intensity of flavor—smoky char combined with light sweetness—that boiled or steamed lobsters can't match. Grilling them meat-side up lets the flesh roast in the shell. There's no way we'd forget the melted butter, but the addition of a sauce packed with herbs adds a fresh dimension to the lobster experience.

3 lobsters (each 1¼ to 1½ pounds)

1 tablespoon plus 1 teaspoon extra-virgin olive oil, plus more for grill

Mixed Herb Sauce (recipe follows)

4 tablespoons unsalted butter, melted

Flaky sea salt, such as Maldon

Mixed fresh herbs, such as mint, flat-leaf parsley, and oregano, coarsely chopped, for serving (optional)

Lemon wedges, for serving

Bring a large pot of water to a boil. Plunge lobsters headfirst into boiling water and cook just until color changes to bright red, about 1 minute. Remove from pot. When cool enough to handle, cut in half lengthwise from head to tail; remove guts.

Heat grill to medium. Lightly oil grates. Drizzle lobsters with oil, then 2 tablespoons mixed herb sauce. Grill, meat-side up, until cooked through, 6 to 8 minutes, then turn once to lightly mark meat. Drizzle with butter, sprinkle with salt and herbs (if desired), and serve with lemon wedges and remaining herb sauce.

Mixed Herb Sauce

MAKES 1½ CUPS

1½ cups fresh flat-leaf parsley leaves

1½ cups fresh mint leaves

¼ cup fresh oregano leaves

¼ cup fresh lemon basil, Thai basil, or lemon balm (optional)

2 garlic cloves, minced

1 teaspoon finely chopped Thai bird chile or other hot chile

2 teaspoons pink peppercorns, crushed

4 anchovy fillets, preferably packed in olive oil, chopped

1 cup extra-virgin olive oil

¼ cup apple cider vinegar

Coarse salt

Pulse herbs, garlic, chile, peppercorns, and anchovies in a food processor until finely chopped. Add oil and pulse to a paste. (Store, covered, up to 4 hours.) Add vinegar and 1 teaspoon salt, and pulse to combine.

Tofu with Ginger-Cilantro Sauce

SERVES 4

We love thick slices of tofu when they're charred to perfection and then brushed with a zesty sauce of cilantro, jalapeño, ginger, and lime. Tofu is ready to eat when you buy it, so a quick stint on the grates is all you need to achieve those coveted grill marks. Serve with rice or rice noodles and a crisp salad.

2 cups fresh cilantro leaves

¼ cup plus 1 tablespoon vegetable oil, plus more for grill

½ jalapeño, seeded and roughly chopped

1 teaspoon finely grated peeled fresh ginger

2 tablespoons fresh lime juice

3 scallions, green parts only, cut into 1-inch pieces

Coarse salt and freshly ground pepper

1 package (14 ounces) extra-firm tofu, drained, pressed, and sliced into 12 pieces (see page 31)

Heat grill to medium. In a food processor, combine cilantro, ¼ cup oil, jalapeño, ginger, lime juice, and scallion greens. Blend ginger-cilantro mixture until smooth; season with salt and pepper.

Brush tofu with 1 tablespoon oil; season with salt and pepper. Lightly oil grates. Grill tofu, turning halfway through, until charred in spots, 4 to 6 minutes. Remove from grill and brush with ginger-cilantro sauce. Serve with remaining sauce on the side.

Out of Hand

We like to approach grilling in an unfussy way,
and if there are no utensils involved, all the better.
Some of our favorite foods get back to fundamentals
and let us eat with our hands—juicy burgers, spicy
tacos, and even sandwiches of all shapes and sizes.
In these pages, along with Martha's favorite beef
burger, you'll find a pork burger with lemongrass,
turkey cheeseburgers, and chickpea sliders. We turn
to Vietnam for a tofu bánh mì, to Korea for short ribs,
and to Mexico for rajas tacos with beans, in addition to
American classics such as fish-and-slaw, pulled pork,
and hearty steak sandwiches.

Steakhouse Burgers

MAKES 4 BURGERS

Grinding your own meat not only allows for the freshest taste, but opens up endless possibilities for custom blends. After much trial and error in our test kitchen, we find this steakhouse-worthy sirloin and short-rib combination contains the optimal proportions of flavor and fat. You can scale this recipe up or down, as long as you use equal parts of each type of meat. A standing mixer's food-grinder attachment makes short work of cubed meat, or ask a butcher to grind a blend for you.

12 ounces boneless short ribs, trimmed of any large pieces of fat

12 ounces sirloin steak, trimmed of any large pieces of fat

Coarse salt and freshly ground pepper

½ medium red onion, cut into ½-inch rounds

Extra-virgin olive oil, for grill and brushing

2 ounces blue cheese, sliced

¼ cup Dijon mustard

¼ cup whole-grain mustard

4 sesame-seed brioche buns, split

Thinly sliced tomatoes and romaine lettuce leaves

Soak wooden skewers, if using, in water 30 minutes.

Cut both meats into small pieces. Grind through large holes of a meat grinder. Combine in a medium bowl, then grind together through small holes of grinder. Gently form into 4 patties. Season with salt.

Heat grill to medium-high. Thread onion slices crosswise onto skewers; brush both sides with oil. Lightly oil grates. Grill onion until tender and lightly charred, about 4 minutes per side. Grill burgers about 2½ minutes per side for medium-rare, placing cheese on burgers in last minute of cooking.

Combine both mustards; set aside. Brush split sides of buns with oil; grill until lightly toasted, about 30 seconds. Season tomato slices with salt and pepper. Sandwich burgers and onions (removed from skewers) between buns with mustard mixture, tomatoes, and lettuce. Serve with additional mustard mixture on the side.

Martha's Favorite Cheeseburgers

MAKES 8 BURGERS

We've grilled literally thousands of hamburgers in the test kitchen, and our food editors have countless opinions: thin or thick patties, pure ground beef or custom blends, toppings galore. In the end, the "perfect burger" is subjective, but this version is Martha's favorite: It calls for fresh horseradish and two types of cheese, melted onto ground chuck burgers, all served on buttered brioche buns.

1½ **cups coarsely grated aged cheddar cheese (4½ ounces)**

1½ **cups coarsely grated aged Swiss cheese (5 ounces)**

5 **teaspoons grated peeled fresh horseradish, or prepared horseradish to taste**

3 **pounds ground beef chuck (85% lean)**

Coarse salt and freshly ground pepper

Vegetable oil, for grill

½ **cup mayonnaise**

3 **tablespoons ketchup**

8 **brioche buns, split**

4 **tablespoons unsalted butter, melted**

8 **slices (¼ inch thick) large, ripe red tomato**

16 **slices crisp-cooked bacon (1 pound)**

8 **lettuce leaves**

Bread-and-butter pickles

Heat grill to medium. Combine both cheeses and horseradish. Gently form beef into 8 patties. Season with salt and pepper. Lightly oil grates. Grill burgers 4 minutes. Flip; top each with just over ¼ cup cheese mixture. Cover grill and cook about 4 minutes more for medium-rare.

Combine mayonnaise and ketchup; set aside. Brush split sides of buns with butter; grill until lightly toasted, about 30 seconds. Season tomato slices with salt and pepper. Sandwich burgers between buns with mayonnaise-and-ketchup mixture, tomato, bacon, lettuce, and pickles.

Turkey-and-Bacon Burgers

MAKES 4 BURGERS

An absolutely irresistible take on a classic, this turkey burger is made from turkey thighs ground with strips of bacon. If you don't have a meat grinder, you can add finely chopped bacon to 1 pound of ground dark turkey meat, or ask your butcher to grind it for you. Because we use the darker thigh meat and combine it with bacon, the burgers are super juicy.

1 pound boneless, skinless turkey thighs, trimmed of fat

7 strips thick-sliced bacon (about 7 ounces)

Coarse salt and freshly ground pepper

Vegetable oil, for grill

3 ounces Swiss cheese, thinly sliced

4 English muffins, split

4 slices tomato

Sliced avocado, romaine lettuce leaves, and mayonnaise

Cut both meats into small pieces. Grind through large holes of a meat grinder. Combine meats in a large bowl, then grind together through small holes of grinder. Gently form into 4 patties. Season with salt.

Heat grill to medium-high, with an indirect-heat zone. Lightly oil grates. Place burgers over direct heat and sear until browned, 1 to 2 minutes per side. Move to indirect heat, and continue grilling until an instant-read thermometer inserted in centers registers 165°F, about 5 minutes per side; place cheese on burgers in last minute of cooking.

Grill English muffins until toasted, about 30 seconds. Season tomato slices with salt and pepper. Sandwich burgers between muffins with tomato, avocado, lettuce, and mayonnaise.

All-Time Favorite Turkey Burgers

MAKES 4 BURGERS

This recipe was developed by the test kitchen back in 2003, and for many at Martha Stewart Living, it's been the go-to turkey burger ever since. Hearty hits of Dijon and grated Gruyère make the patties especially savory, sliced scallions and minced garlic lend bite, and dried breadcrumbs help to bind them together. Get a good sear, then finish over indirect heat until fully cooked. As an alternative to the toppings here, try them with tomato slices, pickles, avocado, and especially bacon.

1½ **pounds ground turkey (preferably 92% to 93% lean)**

½ **cup finely grated Gruyère cheese**

4 **scallions, thinly sliced**

¼ **cup dried breadcrumbs**

¼ **cup Dijon mustard**

1 **garlic clove, minced**

Coarse salt and freshly ground pepper

Vegetable oil, for grill and brushing

4 **whole-wheat buns, split**

Sprouts, sliced red onion, mayonnaise or Aïoli (page 241)

Radish wedges, for serving

Heat grill to high, with an indirect-heat zone. Use a fork to gently combine turkey with cheese, scallions, breadcrumbs, mustard, and garlic in a medium bowl. Add ¾ teaspoon salt and season with pepper. Gently form into 4 patties.

Lightly oil grates. Place burgers over direct heat and sear until browned, 1 to 2 minutes per side. Move patties to indirect heat, and continue grilling until an instant-read thermometer inserted into centers registers 165°F, about 5 minutes per side.

Brush split sides of buns with oil; grill until lightly toasted, about 30 seconds. Sandwich burgers between buns with sprouts, onion, and mayonnaise. Serve with radish wedges.

Chickpea and Lamb Sliders

EACH MAKES 16 SLIDERS

If you're serving meat-eaters and vegetarians alike, keep it simple and grill an assortment of miniature burgers—some lamb, some chickpea—and offer the same toppings (with warm pita bread) for both.

FOR THE CHICKPEA BURGERS

- 1 small (4-inch) pita, torn into bite-size pieces
- 2 cans (15 ounces each) chickpeas, drained and rinsed
- 8 scallions, finely chopped
- ⅔ cup roasted unsalted peanuts or almonds
- 1 teaspoon ground cumin
- 2 tablespoons finely chopped peeled fresh ginger

  Coarse salt and freshly ground pepper
- 2 large eggs

FOR THE LAMB BURGERS

- 1½ pounds ground lamb
- ½ small onion, finely chopped (¼ cup)
- ¼ cup chopped fresh flat-leaf parsley leaves
- 2 teaspoons chopped fresh oregano leaves, or 1 teaspoon dried

  Coarse salt and freshly ground pepper

  Extra-virgin olive oil, for grill and brushing
- 16 small (4-inch) pitas, Yogurt-Cucumber Sauce (page 239), fresh mint leaves, sliced tomatoes, and cucumber spears

Make the chickpea burgers: Soak torn pita in cold water 10 to 15 minutes, then squeeze dry. Combine chickpeas, scallions, soaked pita, peanuts, cumin, and ginger in a food processor; season with salt and pepper. Pulse until coarsely chopped; transfer half the mixture to a medium bowl. Add eggs to food processor and process until smooth; transfer to reserved mixture and combine. Gently form into 16 small patties. Refrigerate until firm, at least 20 minutes or up to overnight.

Make the lamb burgers: Use a fork to gently combine lamb, onion, parsley, and oregano in a medium bowl; season with salt and pepper. Gently form mixture into 16 small patties.

Heat grill to high. Lightly oil grates. Brush each side of burgers generously with oil. Grill chickpea burgers until charred, 3 to 5 minutes per side. Grill lamb burgers 2 to 3 minutes per side for medium-rare.

Warm pitas on grill. Trim 1 end from pita and fill with burgers, Yogurt-Cucumber Sauce, mint, tomatoes, and cucumber.

Smoked-Brisket Sandwiches

MAKES 8 SANDWICHES

The generous amount of fat in brisket makes it the ideal meat to cook low and slow. Brisket can be sold cut into two pieces—the first (or flat) cut and the second (or point) cut. Select a first cut that boasts an even thickness with a cap of fat on one side. We like the multilayered flavor of the sugar-and-spices rub here: It produces tender meat with a deep smokiness and a telltale pink layer—the famed smoke ring— right beneath the charred crust.

1 first-cut beef brisket (5 to 6 pounds), with a layer of fat ¼ to ½ inch thick

2 tablespoons dark-brown sugar

2 tablespoons coarse salt

2 tablespoons chile powder, preferably ancho

2 teaspoons freshly ground pepper

2 teaspoons ground cumin

2 teaspoons dry mustard

8 buns, such as brioche or potato, split

Texas Barbecue Sauce (recipe follows), for serving

Coleslaw, pickles, and potato chips, for serving

Rinse brisket and pat dry with paper towels. Whisk together sugar, salt, chile powder, pepper, cumin, and mustard in a medium bowl. Rub spice mixture evenly all over meat. Wrap in plastic, place in a shallow dish, and refrigerate at least 4 hours but preferably 24 hours. Let sit at room temperature 1 hour before smoking.

Soak dried wood chips (see tip, opposite). Prepare charcoal grill (see page 22), heating coals to whitish-gray; if using a gas grill, heat to medium. Arrange hot coals on opposite ends of bottom grate, leaving center clear. Drain soaked wood chips, and spread evenly on top of coals; let burn until smoking 5 to 10 minutes. Place a disposable 9-by-13-inch aluminum pan in center of bottom grate between coals; fill halfway with water (this creates steam to keep the brisket moist).

Place brisket, fat-side up, in another large, disposable aluminum pan lined with parchment (or use a double sheet of heavy-duty aluminum foil). Place pan with brisket in center of top grate, directly above pan with water. Cover grill, closing all but one vent to maintain temperature between 275°F and 325°F.

Smoke brisket until tender enough to shred with two forks, 7 to 8 hours, basting occasionally. Add 10 to 12 fresh coals to each side of lower grate every hour; for each of the first 3 hours, also add about ¾ cup chips per side.

Remove brisket pan from grill and let stand 15 minutes. Transfer brisket to a cutting board and thinly slice against the grain. Sandwich brisket between buns and serve with Texas Barbecue Sauce, coleslaw, pickles, and potato chips.

Texas Barbecue Sauce

MAKES 8 CUPS

- ¼ teaspoon cumin seeds
- ½ teaspoon coriander seeds
- ⅓ cup vegetable oil
- 3 small Vidalia onions, finely chopped (about 3 cups)
- 6 garlic cloves, minced
  Coarse salt and freshly ground pepper
- 1 tablespoon chile powder, preferably ancho
- ½ cup unsulfured molasses
- ½ cup packed dark-brown sugar
- 4 cups crushed tomatoes (from two 28-ounce cans)
- ¾ cup apple cider vinegar
- ¼ cup distilled white vinegar
- 2 tablespoons Worcestershire sauce

Heat a medium dry skillet over medium-high. Add cumin and coriander seeds, and toast, swirling skillet occasionally, until fragrant, 30 to 60 seconds. Let spices cool, then grind in a spice grinder or clean coffee mill, or with a mortar and pestle.

Heat oil in a medium pot over medium. Add onions and garlic, and cook, stirring occasionally, until translucent and tender, about 10 minutes. Add 1 teaspoon salt, ½ teaspoon pepper, the chile powder, molasses, and brown sugar, and stir to combine. Cook, stirring frequently, until sugar is melted, about 3 minutes. Add tomatoes and cider vinegar, and bring to a simmer. Reduce heat to medium-low and simmer gently, stirring occasionally, until mixture is thick and dark, about 1 hour. (Reduce heat to low if sauce is thickening too quickly.)

Let sauce cool slightly, then puree in a blender. Add 1 tablespoon salt, 1 teaspoon pepper, the white vinegar, and Worcestershire; puree until smooth. With blender running, carefully add 2 cups water in a slow, steady stream. Blend until mixture is smooth and emulsified, adding up to ¼ cup more water if needed. Season with salt and pepper. (Sauce can be refrigerated in an airtight container up to 5 days; let cool completely before storing, and reheat over medium before serving.)

TIP: For gas grills, soak wood chips (1½ cups mesquite, hickory, or other smoked chips) in water for 1 hour prior to grilling—they need to smolder to impart the best flavor. Place them in your grill's smoker box, if it comes equipped with one, or in a disposable pie pan or wrapped in a foil packet with holes poked in the top, and place on the grates. For charcoal grills, put fresh chips directly on the coals. If the chips are dried, soak for 2 hours before placing them on the coals. You'll need to replace the chips, gradually, as they burn out.

Lemongrass Pork Burgers in Lettuce Cups

MAKES 6 BURGERS

The flavors of Southeast Asia were the inspiration for this lean, delicious burger, with an enticing citrusy note of lemongrass and a good dose of ginger. Each petite burger is served inside a lettuce leaf; double-up and layer two leaves for a sturdier cup. Keep these in mind when you want to offer a gluten-free option.

3 shallots, thinly sliced

1½ fresh lemongrass stalks, bottom 6 inches only, finely chopped (6 tablespoons)

1 (2-inch) piece peeled fresh ginger, coarsely chopped

1 pound ground pork

Coarse salt and freshly ground pepper

Vegetable oil, for grill and brushing

Juice of 3 limes (about ¼ cup plus 2 tablespoons)

¼ cup fish sauce

3 to 6 (depending on desired heat) fresh Thai chiles, seeded, if desired, or 1 fresh serrano chile, thinly sliced crosswise

1 head Boston lettuce, leaves separated

Mixed fresh herbs, such as cilantro, mint, Thai basil, lemon basil, and chives

Cucumber spears, for serving

Pulse two-thirds of shallots, the lemongrass, and ginger in a food processor until finely ground. Transfer to a medium bowl. Using your hands, gently combine shallot mixture, pork, 1½ teaspoons salt, and ½ teaspoon pepper (do not overwork meat). Gently form into 6 patties (3 to 4 inches in diameter). Refrigerate, covered, until chilled, at least 1 hour or up to overnight.

Heat grill to medium-high. Lightly oil grates. Brush patties with oil and grill until cooked through, about 5 minutes per side.

Stir together remaining shallots, lime juice, fish sauce, and chiles in a small bowl.

Arrange burgers on lettuce leaves and top with herbs. Serve with cucumber spears and shallot dressing.

Classic Pulled Pork Sandwiches

SERVES 8 TO 12

North Carolina–style pulled pork gets its deep flavor from a dry rub
of sugar, spices, and mustard the night before and then low, slow
cooking (smoked up to eight hours).

FOR THE MEAT

½ boneless pork shoulder (about
  4 pounds), trimmed but with
  a layer of fat

Coarse salt and freshly ground pepper

5 garlic cloves, pressed through
  a garlic press or mashed to a paste

2 tablespoons vegetable oil,
  plus more for grill

1 tablespoon granulated sugar

2 tablespoons light-brown sugar

1 tablespoon sweet paprika

¼ teaspoon dry mustard

¼ teaspoon dried thyme

FOR THE SAUCE

1 cup distilled white vinegar

⅓ cup ketchup

⅓ cup packed light-brown sugar

1 tablespoon coarse salt

¾ teaspoon red-pepper flakes

1 teaspoon freshly ground black pepper

Potato buns, coleslaw, homemade
(page 244) or store-bought, and thinly
sliced cucumber, for serving

Pickles, for serving

Make the meat: Season pork with
2 tablespoons salt. Cover with plastic wrap
and refrigerate overnight. The next day, stir
together garlic and oil. Mix together sugars,
paprika, ¾ teaspoon pepper, mustard,
and thyme. Rub oil mixture over pork,
then sugar mixture. Let stand at room
temperature.

Prepare charcoal grill (see page 22), heating
coals to whitish-gray. Arrange hot coals
on opposite ends of bottom grate, leaving
center clear. Place a disposable 9-by-13-
inch aluminum pan in center of bottom
grate between coals; fill halfway with water
(this creates steam to keep the meat moist).

Place pork on top grate of grill, directly above
pan with water. Cover grill, keeping top and
bottom vents halfway open. Every hour, add
coals (about 16 each time) as needed to keep
grill temperature at a steady 300°F. Cook until
an instant-read thermometer inserted into
thickest part of pork registers about 200°F,
7 to 8 hours. Let meat rest 20 minutes before
pulling it apart with two forks.

Make the sauce: Whisk together all
ingredients in a bowl. Toss pulled pork with
1 cup sauce. Sandwich pork between buns
with coleslaw and cucumber. Serve with
pickles and remaining sauce on the side.

Grilled Ribs with Tangy Barbecue Sauce

SERVES 12

The best thing about this quintessential summer dish is that the ribs take only a few minutes to finish on the grill. Most of the cooking happens in the oven at a low temperature, hours before guests arrive. Brush on the sweet-spicy Tangy Barbecue Sauce at the end, and serve with white bread, coleslaw, charred jalapeños, and sliced onion.

¼ cup plus 1 tablespoon coarse salt

1½ teaspoons freshly ground pepper

3 tablespoons light-brown sugar

3 tablespoons chili powder

4 racks pork spareribs (about 2¼ pounds each), excess fat removed

1½ cups Tangy Barbecue Sauce (page 245)

Vegetable oil, for grill

Sliced white bread, coleslaw, charred jalapeños, and sliced onion, for serving

Preheat oven to 300°F. Mix together salt, pepper, sugar, and chili powder. Rub spice mixture evenly over both sides of ribs. Transfer ribs, bone-side down and slightly overlapping, to 2 rimmed baking sheets. Cover tightly with parchment-lined aluminum foil, and bake until tender, 2½ to 3 hours. (Baked ribs can be refrigerated in an airtight container up to 24 hours; let stand at room temperature 1 hour before grilling.)

Heat grill to medium-high. Divide barbecue sauce in half and reserve half for serving. Lightly oil grates. Transfer ribs to grill, and cook, occasionally turning and brushing with barbecue sauce, until charred, 2 to 5 minutes per side. Transfer to a cutting board and cut between each rib to separate. Serve with reserved barbecue sauce, bread, coleslaw, jalapeños, and sliced onion.

Bistro-Style Chicken Sandwiches

MAKES 4 SANDWICHES

Grilled chicken cutlets make for a no-fuss solution that appeals to just about everybody. Serve them between slices of crusty baguette with grainy mustard, fresh dill, aged cheddar cheese, and crème fraîche. Add a helping of crisp Potato and Green Bean Salad (page 193) on the side for a picnic-worthy combination.

¼ cup plus 3 tablespoons whole-grain mustard

½ cup extra-virgin olive oil, plus more for grill

2 garlic cloves, minced

Coarse salt and freshly ground pepper

2 chicken cutlets (6 ounces each)

4 shallots, unpeeled, halved lengthwise

3 ounces aged cheddar cheese, thinly sliced

3 tablespoons crème fraîche

⅓ cup chopped fresh dill

1 baguette, cut crosswise into 4 pieces, then halved lengthwise

Sour pickles, thinly sliced lengthwise, or cornichons, whole

Mix ¼ cup mustard, the oil, garlic, 1½ teaspoons salt, and ¾ teaspoon pepper in a medium bowl. Add chicken and shallots and toss to coat. Refrigerate, covered, at least 30 minutes and up to 6 hours.

Heat grill to medium-high. Lightly oil grates. Grill shallots, turning occasionally, until softened, 8 to 10 minutes (discard skins). Wipe marinade from chicken, letting excess drip off (discard marinade). Grill chicken until lightly charred and cooked through, 2 to 3 minutes per side. Top with cheese in the last minute of cooking. Halve cutlets.

Combine remaining 3 tablespoons mustard, the crème fraîche, and dill in a small bowl. Spread onto cut sides of baguette pieces. Sandwich chicken between bread with pickles and shallots.

Steak and Charred-Tomato Sandwiches

MAKES 6 SANDWICHES

Grilling steak for a crowd is easy: Start with a sirloin, skirt, or flank cut, cook, slice it thin, then layer it with charred tomatoes and basil leaves on a long loaf. The soft Italian bread soaks up the tomatoes' juices, creating a fresh-off-the-grill steak sandwich beyond compare. Keep the side dishes equally effortless—potato chips and pickles or grilled vegetables.

2 **sirloin, skirt, or flank steaks (about 1¾ pounds each)**

Coarse salt and freshly ground pepper

Extra-virgin olive oil, for grill, brushing, and drizzling

6 **tomatoes, sliced ½-inch thick**

2 **large loaves semisoft Italian bread, halved lengthwise**

Romaine lettuce leaves and fresh basil

Heat grill to high. Season steaks with salt and pepper, and let stand 30 minutes. Lightly oil grates. Grill steaks until an instant-read thermometer inserted into thickest part registers 125°F to 130°F for medium-rare, about 5 minutes per side. Let stand 10 minutes. Thinly slice steaks against the grain.

Meanwhile, drizzle tomato slices with oil; season with salt and pepper. Brush bread with oil. Grill tomatoes until lightly charred and soft, 2 to 4 minutes per side. Grill cut sides of bread until lightly charred, 30 seconds to 2 minutes.

Layer romaine leaves, sliced steak, and grilled tomatoes over bottom halves of bread. Top with basil, drizzle with oil, and season with salt and pepper. Sandwich with top halves of bread. Cut each loaf crosswise into 6 pieces.

New England Fish Sandwiches

MAKES 4 SANDWICHES

The fish sandwich, that staple of New England seaside shacks and southern roadhouses, can be seamlessly treated to the grill instead of frying. Choose a firm-fleshed fish and pat it dry with paper towels to prevent it from sticking—and always scrub those grates clean before grilling. Use metal spatulas to move fish (never use tongs or a grilling fork), turning the fillets only once.

4 cups shredded green cabbage (from ¼ head cabbage)

Coarse salt and freshly ground pepper

1 celery stalk, thinly sliced

1 sweet onion, such as Vidalia or Walla Walla, thinly sliced into rounds

3 tablespoons mayonnaise, plus more for bread (optional)

1 tablespoon red-wine vinegar

¼ teaspoon caraway seeds

Vegetable oil, for grill and brushing

4 skinless striped bass or other firm-fleshed fish fillets (each 4 to 6 ounces)

8 thick slices sandwich bread, such as brioche or country-style white

Toss cabbage with 2 teaspoons salt in a medium bowl; let stand 20 minutes, then press between clean kitchen towels to remove excess liquid. Toss cabbage in a clean medium bowl with celery, half the onion, the mayonnaise, vinegar, and caraway; season with pepper.

Heat grill to medium-high. Lightly oil grates. Pat fish dry with paper towels. Season with salt and pepper, and brush with oil. Grill fish on one side until it is opaque at edges and can be easily turned, 2 to 4 minutes. Turn fish and continue cooking until opaque throughout, 1 to 4 minutes more, depending on thickness. Transfer to a plate.

Grill bread until lightly toasted, 5 to 10 seconds per side. Spread bread with mayonnaise, if desired, and sandwich fish with remaining onion and a generous amount of cabbage slaw.

Salmon Sandwiches with Herbed Mayonnaise

MAKES 4 SANDWICHES

It's worth seeking out wild salmon for its unparalleled flavor. (Ask your fishmonger for salmon that is certified sustainable by organizations such as the Marine Stewardship Council.) Some is flash-frozen, which helps preserve its natural texture, flavor, and nutrition. For fast defrosting, submerge the fish (in its packaging) in a bowl of cold water. It should be ready to cook in about ten minutes. The smoky-sweet rub makes the salmon delicious on its own, but creamy herbed mayo provides a cool contrast.

Vegetable oil, for grill

4 skin-on wild-salmon fillets (each about 6 ounces, 6 inches long, and 1 inch thick)

Extra-virgin olive oil, for rubbing and brushing

1 tablespoon smoked paprika

1 tablespoon light-brown sugar

Coarse salt and freshly ground pepper

¼ cup chopped mixed fresh herbs, such as dill, flat-leaf parsley, basil, and chives

¾ cup mayonnaise

4 seeded rolls, split

Romaine lettuce leaves, sliced tomatoes, and sliced cucumbers

Flaky sea salt, such as Maldon

Heat grill to medium-high. Lightly oil grates. Rub both sides of salmon with olive oil. Stir together paprika, sugar, and 1 teaspoon each coarse salt and pepper; rub over both sides of fish. Brush fish again with olive oil before grilling. Place fish, skin-side down, on grill, and cook until skin no longer sticks and fillets can be easily turned. Turn and continue cooking until center is opaque, 2 to 3 minutes more. Transfer to a plate.

Stir together herbs and mayonnaise. Grill rolls, cut-sides down, until just toasted, about 1 minute. Spread rolls with herbed mayonnaise. Divide salmon among rolls. Top with lettuce, tomatoes, and cucumbers. Season with flaky salt and pepper, and serve.

Tofu Bánh Mì

MAKES 2 SANDWICHES

Tofu's strength is its ability to absorb flavors and act as a foil to strong and spicy ingredients—in this case, the components of a Vietnamese bánh mì (a sandwich made on a baguette, typically with pickled vegetables). First, the tofu is marinated in a Sriracha vinaigrette, then quickly charred and sandwiched between grilled bread. Remember to use extra-firm tofu, which holds up better than soft or firm tofu when grilling.

2 tablespoons fish sauce

¼ cup plus 2 teaspoons unseasoned rice vinegar

1 tablespoon light-brown sugar

1 shallot, thinly sliced

1 teaspoon Sriracha

2 teaspoons grated peeled fresh ginger

12 ounces extra-firm tofu, drained, sliced into ½-inch slabs, and pressed (see page 31)

1 large carrot, cut into matchsticks

4 small radishes, cut into matchsticks

Coarse salt

Extra-virgin olive oil, for grill and brushing

2 (6-inch) baguette pieces, split lengthwise

½ cup fresh cilantro leaves

½ cup fresh mint leaves (optional)

Whisk together fish sauce, ¼ cup vinegar, the sugar, shallot, Sriracha, and ginger. Place tofu in a shallow baking dish or resealable plastic bag. Pour marinade over tofu, cover, and let marinate at room temperature 30 minutes, or up to overnight in the refrigerator.

Meanwhile, in a small bowl, toss carrot and radishes with remaining 2 teaspoons vinegar. Season with salt and refrigerate.

Heat grill to medium-high. Lightly oil grates. Remove tofu from marinade, and pat dry with paper towels; reserve marinade. Grill tofu until crisp and charred in spots, 2 to 3 minutes per side.

Generously brush cut sides of baguette with olive oil. Grill bread, cut-side down, until toasted and golden, about 1 minute. Sandwich grilled tofu between bread with carrot and radish mixture, herbs, and a drizzle of reserved marinade.

Chile-Rubbed Flank Steak Tacos

MAKES 12 TACOS

Flank steak works well for grilling because it's flavorful, affordable, and a large cut can be sliced to feed a small crowd. Serve these tacos with tomatillo salsa, and add toppings such as chopped fresh jalapeño or serrano chiles and shredded Monterey Jack or crumbled Cotija cheeses. The salsa calls for fresh tomatillos—look for firm fruit covered with tight husks—but you can also roast them over direct heat until soft, about eight minutes.

FOR THE SALSA

- ¼ pound tomatillos (about 2 medium), husked, rinsed, and finely chopped
- ¼ cup finely chopped red onion
- 1 jalapeño, seeded and finely chopped

  Coarse salt

FOR THE TACOS

- 1 tablespoon vegetable oil, plus more for grill
- 2 tablespoons chile powder, such as ancho, pasilla, or chipotle
- 2 tablespoons light-brown sugar
- 2 tablespoons soy sauce
- 2 tablespoons fresh lime juice, plus wedges for serving
- 1½ pounds flank steak

  Coarse salt and freshly ground pepper

- 1 large red onion, cut into ¼-inch rounds

  Warmed corn tortillas and cilantro sprigs, for serving

Make the salsa: In a small bowl, combine tomatillos, onion, and jalapeño. Season with salt and let stand at least 10 minutes before serving. (Salsa can be refrigerated in an airtight container up to 3 days.)

Make the tacos: In another small bowl, whisk together oil, chile powder, sugar, soy sauce, and lime juice. Place steak in a shallow baking dish or resealable plastic bag. Pour marinade over steak; turn to coat. Cover and let marinate in refrigerator at least 1 hour or up to 24 hours.

Heat grill to medium-high. Lightly oil grates. Remove steak from marinade, and pat dry with paper towels; reserve marinade. Season steak with salt and pepper. Grill onion and steak, turning occasionally, until onion is lightly charred and steak is medium-rare, about 10 minutes. Brush onion and steak with reserved marinade, and cook about 1 minute more, turning once. Place onion on a serving plate. Transfer steak to a cutting board and let rest 10 minutes before thinly slicing it against the grain. Serve steak and onion with tortillas, salsa, lime wedges, and cilantro.

Fish Tacos with Shredded Cabbage

MAKES 12 TACOS

Popular Baja-style fish tacos feature double-fried fillets, but we prefer to rub a whole fish with three spices and then grill it. Try a tender, flaky variety, such as red snapper or striped bass. Pickled jalapeños, carrots, and red onions are a staple at taco stands—you can make the spicy-sweet combo while the fish is marinating or even a few days ahead. Look for authentic crema at Latin markets, or thin 1 cup sour cream with about 1 tablespoon lime juice and 1 tablespoon water.

2 teaspoons ground cumin

2 tablespoons dried oregano

2 tablespoons chile powder, such as ancho or pasilla

Coarse salt

½ cup vegetable oil, plus more for grill

¼ cup finely chopped fresh cilantro, plus sprigs for serving

1 (2½-pound) whole fish, such as striped bass or red snapper, cleaned, head and tail left intact

5 cups shredded green cabbage (½ medium cabbage, about 12 ounces)

Lime wedges, warmed white corn tortillas, Pickled Vegetables (page 244), and crema or sour cream, for serving

Stir together spices and 1 tablespoon salt. Mix in oil and cilantro to make a loose paste. Use a sharp knife to make shallow (¼ inch) diagonal slashes about 1½ inches apart on both sides of fish skin; transfer fish to a large dish and rub both sides with spice mixture. Refrigerate at least 30 minutes or up to 4 hours.

Meanwhile, toss together cabbage and 1½ teaspoons salt in a medium bowl. Let stand 30 minutes, then squeeze between clean kitchen towels to remove excess liquid.

Heat grill to medium-high. Lightly oil grates. Grill fish until underside is lightly charred and flesh along slashes turns opaque, 10 to 15 minutes, then turn using two metal spatulas. Cook until charred and opaque in slashes, about 10 minutes more.

Transfer fish to a platter; let cool slightly. Using a fork, flake fish into bite-size pieces. Garnish platter with lime wedges and cilantro sprigs. Serve with cabbage, tortillas, pickled vegetables, crema, and cilantro.

Grilled Pork Tacos al Pastor

MAKES 24 TACOS

This recipe first came to us from Chef Rick Bayless of Chicago.
For him, it is reminiscent of the fabulous Mexican street vendors who
shave off pieces of marinated pork, add charred pineapple, and place
it all in a warm tortilla. For us, it's pure satisfaction, no matter
where you are in the world.

1 package (3½ ounces) achiote paste

3 chipotle chiles in adobo sauce (from 1 can), plus ¼ cup sauce

¼ cup vegetable oil, plus more for grill and brushing

1½ pounds boneless pork shoulder, about 1¼ inch thick

1 medium red onion, sliced into ½-inch rounds

Coarse salt

½ pineapple (about 12 ounces), peeled and sliced into ¼-inch rounds

Corn tortillas, warmed, for serving

Smoky Chipotle Salsa (page 244), for serving

Lime wedges, fresh cilantro leaves, and plantain chips, for serving

In a blender, combine achiote paste, chiles plus sauce, oil, and ¾ cup water; blend until smooth, about 5 seconds. Place pork in a shallow baking dish or resealable plastic bag. Pour one-third of marinade over pork; turn to coat. (Refrigerate remaining marinade up to 1 month, to use on other meat or fish.) Cover pork and let marinate in refrigerator at least 1 hour or up to 2 days.

Remove pork from marinade, letting excess drip off (discard marinade).

Heat grill to medium-high, with an indirect-heat zone. Lightly oil grates. Grill pork over direct heat until browned and sizzling, about 15 minutes per side. Wrap in parchment-lined aluminum foil and transfer to indirect heat; cook until tender when pressed, about 30 minutes.

Meanwhile, brush onion slices with oil, and season with salt. Arrange in a single layer over direct heat. Cook until grill marks are dark, about 2 minutes per side. Move to indirect heat and cook until soft, 5 to 8 minutes. Repeat with pineapple.

Transfer pork to a cutting board and thinly slice. Add to a skillet set on grill to keep warm. Chop onion and pineapple into small pieces, add to skillet, and toss to combine. Season with salt.

Serve pork mixture with tortillas, Smoky Chipotle Salsa, lime wedges, and cilantro.

Fire-Roasted Rajas Tacos with Beans

SERVES 6

Grilled poblano chiles add smoky flavor to countless Mexican dishes. They're often cut into strips, called *rajas,* and combined with roasted or grilled onions. (Use a grill basket, if you have one, to avoid food falling into the flames.) We've added tomatoes, too, for full-bodied vegetarian tacos. Cotija cheese contributes a salty, fresh flavor, but you can substitute other crumbled cheeses such as feta.

- 1 tablespoon vegetable oil, plus more for grill and brushing
- 1¼ pounds large tomatoes (about 2), halved crosswise
- 1 large white onion, sliced into ½-inch rounds
- 2 poblano chiles
- 4 large garlic cloves, unpeeled
- 1 tablespoon fresh lime juice, or to taste
- 2 tablespoons coarsely chopped fresh cilantro
- Coarse salt and freshly ground pepper
- ½ teaspoon cumin seeds
- 2 cups canned beans, such as red, black, or pinto
- Warmed corn tortillas, crumbled Cotija cheese, and sliced radishes, for serving

Heat grill to medium. Lightly oil grates. Lightly brush cut sides of tomatoes with oil and place, cut-side down, on grill or in grill basket, along with onion, poblanos, and 3 garlic cloves. Grill vegetables, turning occasionally, until softened and blackened in spots, about 10 minutes for garlic, 15 minutes for poblanos, and 20 minutes for tomatoes and onion. When vegetables are cool enough to handle, remove skins from tomatoes and garlic. Coarsely chop tomatoes and onion, and transfer with garlic to a food processor; pulse until coarsely pureed. Transfer salsa mixture to a large bowl, reserving about ½ cup for beans.

Remove stems and seeds from poblanos and wipe with a paper towel to remove skin; slice into thin strips. Add strips to large bowl with salsa mixture, along with lime juice and cilantro. Stir to combine, and season with salt and pepper.

Peel and finely chop remaining garlic clove. Heat a medium skillet over medium. Add cumin, and cook, stirring, until fragrant and browned, 30 seconds to 1 minute. Add oil and chopped garlic, and cook until fragrant and barely golden, about 1 minute. Stir in beans and season with salt. Cook until heated through, about 5 minutes, mashing slightly with the back of a spoon. Add reserved salsa and stir to combine.

Serve poblanos and beans with tortillas, Cotija, and radishes.

Korean Short Ribs

SERVES 6

These gingery ribs, called *kalbi,* are made with flanken-style short ribs, which means they are cut across the rib bones, and have a thin strip of meat and smaller bones within. Flanken-style ribs cook rapidly over high heat, so they need to be watched carefully. As counterpoints, kimchi adds bright acidity while the red chile paste gochujang provides just the right amount of mellow heat; both can be found at many grocers. You can find flanken-style ribs at some Asian grocers, or ask a butcher to cut them for you.

3 tablespoons soy sauce

1 tablespoon unseasoned rice vinegar

1 tablespoon light-brown sugar

1 teaspoon finely grated peeled fresh ginger

1 teaspoon sesame seeds

1 teaspoon minced garlic

2 tablespoons thinly sliced scallions, plus more for serving

1½ pounds bone-in Korean-style flanken short ribs, ¼ inch thick

Vegetable oil, for grill

Kimchi, gochujang paste, sliced cucumbers, and Bibb lettuce, for serving

Combine soy sauce, vinegar, sugar, ginger, sesame seeds, garlic, and scallions in a shallow dish. Add ribs and turn to coat. Cover and refrigerate at least 8 hours or up to overnight.

Heat grill to medium-high. Lightly oil grates. Grill ribs until cooked through, 2 to 3 minutes per side. Serve with kimchi, gochujang paste, sliced cucumbers and scallions, and lettuce.

On a Platter

When you have a small crowd to feed, or perhaps just your family, one big platter overflowing with delicious options—main dish and sides together—is an easy way to present the meal beautifully. The approach can be casual, as in a salad of flaked grilled salmon, smoky sugar snap peas, potatoes, and hard-cooked eggs, on a bed of lemony watercress. Or it can be more formal, showcasing a tender porterhouse steak plated center stage and surrounded by paprika potatoes, sweet onions, and crisp romaine wedges. Either way, a meal passed on a platter encourages simplicity, sharing, and conviviality—all the things we love about the grilling season.

Chicken and Pea Salad with Dijon Vinaigrette

SERVES 8 TO 10

If you're looking for a platter to make ahead, this salad of smoky charred chicken (featuring both light and dark meat) with bright peas, herbs, and butterhead lettuce is it. You can grill the chicken up to a day ahead; refrigerate until about an hour before serving, then let it come to room temperature while you prepare the rest of the salad.

¾ cup extra-virgin olive oil, plus more for grill

Juice of 3 to 4 lemons (about ⅓ cup plus 2 tablespoons)

1 tablespoon plus 1 teaspoon minced garlic (about 4 cloves)

Coarse salt and freshly ground pepper

5 boneless, skinless chicken breast halves (3 to 3½ pounds)

12 chicken drumsticks (about 4½ pounds)

2 cups peas, preferably fresh

2 tablespoons finely chopped shallot

2 tablespoons Dijon mustard

½ cup chopped fresh mint leaves, plus ½ cup whole fresh mint leaves

1 to 2 heads butterhead lettuce, such as Bibb, leaves separated

Whisk together ¼ cup oil, 2 tablespoons lemon juice, and 1 tablespoon garlic; season with salt and pepper. Place chicken in a large shallow baking dish or resealable plastic bag, and cover with marinade. Refrigerate, covered, at least 2 hours or up to overnight.

Cook peas in a pot of boiling water until just tender, 2 to 3 minutes. Drain and submerge in ice water.

Heat grill to medium-high, with an indirect-heat zone. Remove chicken from marinade and pat dry with paper towels (discard marinade). Lightly oil grates. Place chicken over indirect heat. Cover grill and cook, turning occasionally, until pieces are cooked through and an instant-read thermometer inserted into thickest parts (avoiding bone) registers 165°F, about 20 minutes for breasts and 30 minutes for drumsticks. Uncover grill and transfer chicken to direct heat. Cook, turning once, until lightly charred, 3 to 4 minutes. Before serving, slice chicken breasts.

Whisk remaining ⅓ cup lemon juice, 1 teaspoon garlic, the shallot, mustard, 1 teaspoon salt, and chopped mint in a medium bowl; pour remaining ½ cup oil in a steady stream, whisking constantly until combined. Arrange lettuce, whole mint leaves, and peas on a serving platter. Toss chicken in dressing and arrange on salad. Pour remaining dressing over salad.

Grilled Chicken and Sausage with Leeks, Shallots, and Onions

SERVES 6 TO 8

Fresh alliums—a rich assortment of onions, shallots, and leeks—develop a smoky sweetness on the grill, and become playful companions for grilled sausage and chicken. Snipped chive flowers, if you have them, are just the right garnish.

12 bone-in chicken pieces, such as drumsticks, thighs, or breasts halved crosswise (4½ to 5 pounds)

8 garlic cloves, smashed

   Coarse salt and freshly ground pepper

¼ cup snipped fresh chives (½ bunch), plus flowers for garnish (optional)

¼ cup plus 2 tablespoons Dijon mustard

¼ cup extra-virgin olive oil, plus more for grill and drizzling

6 to 8 assorted onions and shallots, halved or quartered if large

4 leeks, trimmed, leaving root ends intact, halved lengthwise, and rinsed

2 tablespoons sherry vinegar

2 pounds sausage, preferably chicken

   Butter lettuce leaves, for serving

Cut two ¼-inch-deep slashes across the skin side of each piece of chicken. Puree garlic, 1½ teaspoons salt, and the chives in a food processor until a smooth paste forms. Transfer to a medium bowl, stir in mustard and oil, and season with pepper. Rub mixture onto chicken, including under the skin. Cover and refrigerate at least 2 hours or up to overnight.

Heat grill to medium, with an indirect-heat zone. Thread onions and shallots onto skewers. Lightly drizzle onions, shallots, and leeks with oil, and season with salt and pepper. Lightly oil grates. Grill vegetables until lightly charred and tender, about 25 minutes for leeks and 45 minutes for onions and shallots. Drizzle vegetables with 1 tablespoon vinegar while warm.

Meanwhile, working in batches, place chicken over indirect heat. Cover grill and cook, turning occasionally, until cooked through and an instant-read thermometer inserted into thickest parts (avoiding bone) registers 165°F, 30 to 35 minutes. Uncover grill and transfer chicken to direct heat. Cook, turning once, until lightly charred, 3 to 4 minutes. Drizzle with remaining vinegar while warm.

Place sausage on a clean, lightly oiled section of grill, over direct heat. Grill until golden brown, 6 to 7 minutes. Turn and continue to grill until cooked through, 6 to 8 minutes more. Serve chicken, sausages, and grilled vegetables on lettuce leaves. Garnish with chive flowers, if desired.

Chicken with Cucumber, Radish, and Cherry Tomato Relish

SERVES 6

Boneless, skinless chicken breast halves are a grilling staple. Tailor-made for busy evenings, they cook quickly and pair readily with all kinds of seasonal accompaniments. This crunchy, colorful vegetable medley gets a nice addition of heat from a jalapeño-infused vinegar; while the chicken cooks, the relish steeps until lightly pickled. Fresh mint leaves provide an aromatic finishing touch.

¼ cup white-wine vinegar, plus more for drizzling

1 teaspoon sugar

2 garlic cloves, smashed

1 small jalapeño, seeded and quartered

Coarse salt and freshly ground pepper

1 English cucumber (12 ounces), peeled and cut into ¼-inch pieces

5 radishes, thinly sliced

8 ounces cherry tomatoes, halved, or quartered if large

1 small red onion, finely chopped

6 boneless, skinless chicken breast halves (about 2 pounds)

Vegetable oil, for grill

1 cup fresh mint, torn into ½-inch pieces, plus sprigs for serving

Bring vinegar, ¼ cup water, the sugar, garlic, jalapeño, and ¾ teaspoon salt to a boil in a small saucepan. Remove from heat and let stand 15 minutes. Strain through a fine-mesh sieve (discard solids). Let cool completely.

Combine cucumber, radishes, tomatoes, and onion in a medium bowl. Pour in vinegar mixture and toss to coat. Let stand at least 10 minutes and up to 1 day.

Heat grill to medium-high. Season chicken with salt and pepper. Lightly oil grates. Working in batches, grill chicken until cooked through, 6 to 7 minutes per side. Transfer to a platter and let rest 10 minutes. Meanwhile, stir mint into relish. Season relish with salt and pepper, and drizzle with vinegar. Spoon over chicken and serve garnished with mint sprigs.

Citrus-Chile Turkey Breast

SERVES 8

Slow-cooked turkey breast marinated in a robust sauce of Mexican chiles and mixed citrus creates a meltingly tender centerpiece. Corn on the cob is prepared as street vendors in Mexico cook *elote asado*— grilled until charred, then rubbed with crema and sprinkled with salty Cotija cheese. This version uses a pantry staple, mayonnaise, in lieu of the traditional crema; you could also use sour cream.

12 **dried cascabel chiles (about 2 ounces) or 5 ancho chiles (dried poblanos)**

Juice of 2 oranges

Juice of 1 lime

5 **garlic cloves**

1 **small white onion, chopped**

Coarse salt

1 **boneless, skinless turkey breast half (about 3 pounds)**

Vegetable oil, for grill and brushing

4 **fresh poblano chiles**

4 **ears corn, shucked**

Mayonnaise, for brushing

½ **cup crumbled Cotija cheese**

Sprigs of oregano, for serving

Toast cascabels in a dry skillet over medium heat, turning occasionally, until slightly softened, about 5 minutes. Let cool slightly, then remove seeds and ribs. Place chiles in a small bowl and cover with boiling water. Let stand 15 minutes; drain. Transfer chiles to a blender. Add both juices, the garlic, onion, and 1 teaspoon salt; blend until smooth (you'll have about 1 cup).

Rub turkey with ¼ cup sauce. (Reserve remaining sauce; refrigerate.) Cover turkey in plastic wrap and refrigerate at least 2 hours or up to overnight. Let turkey and reserved sauce stand at room temperature 30 minutes before grilling. Wipe off excess marinade and lightly brush with oil.

Heat grill to medium, with an indirect-heat zone. Lightly oil grates. Place turkey over indirect heat and cook, covered, until an instant-read thermometer inserted into thickest part registers 165°F, 1 to 1½ hours. Transfer to a cutting board; let rest 15 to 30 minutes before slicing.

Meanwhile, increase heat to medium-high. Grill fresh poblanos, turning occasionally until charred and softened, about 15 minutes. Brush corn with oil and season with salt. Arrange on grill, parallel with the grates. Grill corn, turning occasionally, until kernels are lightly charred and tender, 10 to 15 minutes; transfer to a platter. Brush with mayonnaise and sprinkle with Cotija.

Serve sliced turkey, grilled corn, and poblanos garnished with oregano and reserved sauce on the side.

Ginger-Soy Pork Chops with Bok Choy

SERVES 4

This take on the Southern go-to meal of pork chops and greens features savory ginger-glazed chops. Instead of long-simmered greens like collards, they are served with wedges of slightly crunchy bok choy. High-heat grilling gets this platter passing around the table in about 30 minutes. Serve the pork chops at the center, surrounded by the bok choy, with a bowl of seasoned rice.

1 **cup long-grain white rice**

2 **tablespoons unseasoned rice vinegar**

¼ **teaspoon red-pepper flakes**

Coarse salt and freshly ground black pepper

2 **tablespoons honey**

1 **teaspoon soy sauce**

1 **teaspoon finely grated peeled fresh ginger**

4 **bone-in pork chops (each 8 to 10 ounces and 1 inch thick)**

Vegetable oil, for grill

4 **heads baby bok choy, halved lengthwise**

1 **tablespoon toasted sesame oil**

Cook rice according to package instructions. With a fork, stir in vinegar and red-pepper flakes. Season with salt. Cover to keep warm.

Heat grill to high. Combine honey, soy sauce, and ginger in a small bowl.

Season pork chops with salt and black pepper. Lightly oil grates. Grill pork, turning once, until an instant-read thermometer inserted into thickest parts (avoiding bone) registers 138°F to 145°F for medium, 5 to 7 minutes per side. Brush pork with honey-soy glaze and grill until glaze caramelizes, about 30 seconds more per side. Transfer pork to a platter to rest 5 to 10 minutes.

Place bok choy in a shallow bowl and drizzle with sesame oil. Season with salt and black pepper, and toss to coat. Grill until lightly charred on both sides, 2 to 3 minutes per side. Transfer to platter with chops and serve with rice.

Porterhouse Steaks with Paprika Potatoes and Lemony Romaine Wedges

SERVES 6

Here's a casual take on the steakhouse dinner, all the elements are served family-style: porterhouse steaks, paprika-dusted potatoes, sweet onions, and romaine wedges drizzled with a creamy lemon dressing.

- 2 **bone-in porterhouse steaks, each 1½ to 1¾ pounds and 1½ inches thick**

  Coarse salt and freshly ground pepper
- 2½ **pounds new potatoes, scrubbed**

  Zest of 2 lemons plus juice of 1 lemon
- 2 **small garlic cloves, minced**
- ½ **cup mayonnaise**
- ½ **cup extra-virgin olive oil, plus more for grill and brushing**
- 2 **sweet onions, such as Vidalia, sliced into ½-inch rounds**
- 1 **teaspoon Worcestershire sauce**
- 1 **tablespoon white-wine vinegar**
- 1 **teaspoon pimentón (smoked paprika)**
- 2 **heads romaine lettuce, cut lengthwise into wedges**
- 2 **tablespoons snipped fresh chives**

Sprinkle steaks with 1 teaspoon salt and season with pepper. Let stand 30 minutes to 1 hour.

Cover potatoes by 2 inches of water in a medium saucepan; add 1 tablespoon salt. Bring to a boil, reduce to a simmer, and cook until just tender, 10 to 15 minutes. Drain, let cool slightly, and halve (or quarter if large).

Whisk together lemon zest and juice, garlic, and mayonnaise in a small bowl. Gradually whisk in oil. Season with salt and pepper, and reserve for romaine wedges.

Heat grill to medium-high. Brush both sides of onion rounds with oil. Season with salt and pepper. Using a grill basket or skewers, grill onions until tender, about 8 minutes. Transfer to a medium bowl, and toss with Worcestershire and vinegar. Season with salt and pepper.

Lightly oil grates. Pat steaks dry and brush lightly with oil. Grill until an instant-read thermometer inserted into thickest parts (avoiding bone) registers 125°F to 130°F for medium-rare, 6 to 7 minutes per side. Using tongs, sear steaks on edges, about 1 minute per side. Transfer to a cutting board and let rest 10 minutes.

Brush potatoes with oil, and grill until golden and crisp, 8 to 10 minutes. Season with salt and sprinkle with pimentón.

Season romaine with salt and pepper. Drizzle with dressing and sprinkle with chives. Slice steaks and arrange on platter, with onions, potatoes, and romaine wedges.

Honey-Glazed Pork Tenderloin with Grilled Apricots

SERVES 4

The key to cooking delicate tenderloin on the grill is to brown it quickly over direct heat, then finish over indirect, but for only about 10 minutes, to prevent it from becoming dry. An aromatic honey glaze, brushed on at the end, unites the pork and fresh apricots.

- 1 teaspoon coriander seeds
- ½ teaspoon black peppercorns
- 1 (2-inch) piece peeled fresh ginger, thinly sliced
- ¾ cup honey
- 2 tablespoons apple cider vinegar

    Coarse salt and freshly ground pepper

- 1 pork tenderloin (1¼ pounds)

    Olive oil, for grill and brushing

- 8 scallions
- 6 medium-ripe apricots (about 1 pound), halved and pitted

Using a mortar and pestle, coarsely crush coriander seeds and peppercorns. Toast in a small dry saucepan over medium heat, shaking pan occasionally, until fragrant and lightly browned, 1 to 2 minutes. Add ginger, honey, vinegar, and ¼ teaspoon salt, and cook until bubbling rapidly, about 5 minutes. Remove from heat and let stand 15 minutes; strain through a fine-mesh sieve into a small bowl (discard solids).

Heat grill to high, with an indirect-heat zone. Season pork with ½ teaspoon salt and pepper to taste. Brush pork with oil. Lightly oil grates. Grill pork until browned, about 3 minutes per side. Transfer to indirect heat, and cook until an instant-read thermometer inserted into thickest part registers 138°F to 145°F for medium, 10 to 12 minutes more. Remove pork from grill and spoon 2 to 3 tablespoons of glaze on top. Let rest 10 minutes.

Meanwhile, season scallions with salt and brush with oil; grill until lightly charred and tender, about 3 minutes. Generously brush apricots with oil. Grill, cut-side down, until grill marks appear and apricots can be turned without sticking, about 3 minutes. Turn and cook until flesh is tender when pressed, about 2 minutes more. Slice pork and arrange on platter with scallions and apricots. Drizzle remaining glaze over apricots, scallions, and pork.

Sirloin Skewers with Zucchini, Mint, and Rice

SERVES 4

A platter of lean beef sirloin, rice, and garden zucchini is a healthy meal you can take from kitchen to grill to table in under an hour. While the rice is cooking, the steak and zucchini can share grill space to be done at the same time. A scattering of mint and red-pepper flakes, plus fresh lime, brings a final brightness to the dish.

1 cup short-grain brown rice

3 scallions, thinly sliced crosswise

8 ounces sirloin steak, cut into 1½-inch cubes

2 medium zucchini, halved crosswise and cut into spears

Coarse salt and freshly ground black pepper

Extra-virgin olive oil, for grill and drizzling

½ cup fresh mint leaves

½ teaspoon red-pepper flakes

Lime wedges, for serving

Soak 4 wooden skewers, if using, in water 30 minutes.

Bring rice and 2 cups water to a boil. Reduce heat to a simmer and cover. Cook rice until tender and water is absorbed, about 45 minutes. Let stand, covered, 5 minutes. Fluff with a fork. Stir in scallions.

Heat grill to medium-high. Thread beef onto skewers. Season beef and zucchini with salt and black pepper; drizzle with oil. Lightly oil grates. Grill beef and zucchini, turning occasionally, until cooked through and blackened in parts, 6 to 8 minutes for each. Transfer rice to a platter, and arrange beef and zucchini on top. Scatter with mint leaves and red-pepper flakes. Serve with lime wedges.

Lamb Kebabs with Naan, Cilantro Chutney, and Raita

SERVES 6

All the elements are here for an Indian-inspired grilled feast: Just slide bites of curry-yogurt-marinated lamb straight from the skewer onto warm pieces of naan, then top with bright cilantro chutney and a dollop of cool raita. Serve with grilled baby eggplants and Indian pickles on the side.

2 pounds boneless leg of lamb, cut into 1½-inch pieces

1 cup whole-milk yogurt, preferably Greek-style

Zest of ½ lime plus 1 tablespoon fresh juice

½ teaspoon honey

½ teaspoon curry powder

½ teaspoon ground coriander

2 tablespoons finely chopped onion

2 tablespoons coarsely chopped fresh mint leaves

Coarse salt and freshly ground pepper

6 baby eggplants

Vegetable oil, for grill and brushing

Naan, for serving

2 tablespoons unsalted butter, room temperature

Cilantro Chutney with Coconut and Lime and Cucumber Raita (page 243), for serving

Soak 6 wooden skewers, if using, in water 30 minutes.

Place lamb in a shallow baking dish or resealable plastic bag. Stir together yogurt, lime zest and juice, honey, curry powder, coriander, onion, and mint in a medium bowl. Season with salt and pepper. Pour marinade over lamb mixture; toss to coat. Cover and let marinate in refrigerator at least 6 hours or up to overnight. Remove from marinade and pat dry with paper towels (discard marinade).

Thread lamb onto 3 skewers. Season with salt and pepper. Thread eggplant onto 3 skewers, season with salt, and brush with oil.

Heat grill to medium-high. Lightly oil grates. Grill eggplants, turning frequently, until charred on outside and flesh has collapsed, 8 to 10 minutes. Grill lamb until browned on all sides, 3 to 4 minutes per side for medium. Grill naan until lightly charred on both sides; brush with butter.

Serve lamb, eggplants, and naan with cilantro chutney and cucumber raita.

Salmon Salad with Sugar Snap Peas, Eggs, and Potatoes

SERVES 8

On a hot summer day, a niçoise-inspired main-course salad (with grilled salmon, eight-minute eggs, fresh sugar snap peas, watercress, and boiled potatoes) is a reliable crowd-pleaser that looks stunning arranged on a platter or tossed in a serving bowl. When grilled, the naturally sweet sugar snaps take on a smoky flavor.

8 anchovy fillets, preferably packed in olive oil, drained

1 teaspoon Dijon mustard

1 teaspoon lemon zest plus 3 tablespoons fresh juice (from 1 to 2 lemons)

½ cup plus 2 teaspoons extra-virgin olive oil, plus more for grill and brushing

Coarse salt and freshly ground pepper

12 ounces small boiling potatoes, such as fingerling, scrubbed

6 large eggs

1¼ pounds skin-on salmon fillet (about 1¾ inches at thickest part)

12 ounces sugar snap peas

3 cups watercress

Mash anchovies with a spoon in a small bowl. Add mustard and 2 tablespoons lemon juice. Gradually whisk in ½ cup oil. Season with salt and pepper, and reserve.

Cover potatoes by 2 inches of water in a pot. Add 1 tablespoon salt. Bring to a boil, reduce to a simmer, and cook until tender, about 12 minutes; drain. Let stand until cool enough to handle, then halve potatoes.

Meanwhile, bring another pot of water to a boil. Gently lower eggs into pot and simmer 8 minutes. Drain, then run under cold water to stop cooking; peel and halve.

Heat grill to medium-high. Brush salmon lightly with oil, sprinkle with zest and remaining tablespoon lemon juice, and season with salt and pepper. Lightly oil grates. Grill salmon, skin-side down, until skin is crisp and browned, about 6 minutes per side for medium-rare, 8 minutes per side for medium.

Toss snap peas with remaining 2 teaspoons oil. Using a grill basket, grill peas, tossing frequently, until charred in spots, 3 to 5 minutes.

Pour half of reserved dressing into a serving bowl. Add potatoes and toss to coat. Add watercress and toss again. Flake salmon into large pieces and add to bowl. Top with eggs and peas. Serve with remaining dressing on the side.

Striped Bass with Clam Chowder

SERVES 4

This pot of chowder may not be a traditional platter, but it is an all-in-one dish perfect for late-summer entertaining. Striped bass is also sold as striper; you can substitute it with other firm, white-flesh fish, such as black sea bass. Here, we serve the fillets over corn-and-clam chowder; they're also delicious with just a sprinkling of lemon juice.

- 4 dozen Manila or littleneck clams (about 2 pounds), scrubbed
- ½ cup dry white wine
- 1 tablespoon unsalted butter
- 2 shallots, thinly sliced
- 1 celery stalk, thinly sliced
- 2 Yukon Gold or russet potatoes, scrubbed and cut into ¾-inch pieces
- 2 cups fresh corn kernels (about 3 ears)
- 1 sprig thyme
- 1 fresh bay leaf
- 1 cup heavy cream
- 4 skin-on striped bass fillets (each about 6 ounces)

  Extra-virgin olive oil, for grill and brushing

  Coarse salt and freshly ground pepper

  Lemon wedges and oyster crackers, for serving

Place clams and wine in a large saucepan. Cover and cook over medium heat until clams open, 6 to 8 minutes. Using a slotted spoon, transfer clams to a large bowl (discard any that don't open). Strain cooking liquid through a fine-mesh sieve into a small bowl, leaving grit and sand behind; reserve cooking liquid.

Rinse saucepan. Melt butter over medium heat. Add shallots and celery, and cook until softened, about 4 minutes. Add potatoes, corn, thyme, and bay leaf. Add cream and reserved clam cooking liquid, and stir to combine. Cover, reduce heat to medium-low, and simmer until potatoes are tender, about 20 minutes. Arrange clams on top of chowder. Cover and continue cooking until just heated through, about 5 minutes.

Meanwhile, heat grill to medium-high. Brush fish with oil, and season with salt and pepper. Lightly oil grates. Grill fish, skin-side down, until skin is lightly browned and starting to crisp. Turn fillets and cook until well browned (center will be opaque), 5 to 6 minutes more.

Remove chowder from heat, and season with salt and pepper. Add fish to chowder and spoon some soup over fish. Serve with lemon wedges and oyster crackers.

Caesar Salad with Mojo-Marinated Shrimp

SERVES 4

One of the most refreshing platters around is a Cuban-inspired Caesar with twists of citrus. Cuban mojo marinade is typically made with the tart juice from sour oranges, such as Sevilles. Because sour oranges are not always available, we re-created that flavor with a mixture of regular orange juice and lime juice.

FOR THE MARINADE

2 teaspoons orange zest plus ½ cup fresh juice (from 1 to 2 oranges)

3 tablespoons fresh lime juice

¼ cup extra-virgin olive oil

2 tablespoons chopped fresh oregano

1 garlic clove, minced

Coarse salt and freshly ground pepper

FOR THE SALAD

1½ pounds jumbo shrimp (about 12), peeled and deveined (tails left on)

½ baguette, halved lengthwise

¼ cup plus 1 tablespoon extra-virgin olive oil, plus more for grill and brushing

Coarse salt and freshly ground pepper

2 heads crisp small lettuce leaves, such as romaine hearts or baby gem

1 firm, ripe avocado, halved, pitted, and cut into ½-inch cubes

Caesar Dressing (page 244)

¼ cup grated Parmigiano-Reggiano cheese (about 1 ounce)

Make the marinade: Whisk together orange zest and juice, lime juice, oil, oregano, and garlic. Add 1 teaspoon salt and season with pepper. Cover and refrigerate up to 24 hours.

Make the salad: Mix shrimp and ⅔ cup mojo marinade in a medium bowl; reserve remaining marinade. Cover and let stand 20 minutes.

Heat grill to high. Brush both sides of baguette halves with oil, and season with salt and pepper. Lightly oil grates. Grill bread until toasted, about 1 minute per side. Let cool. Cut into 1-inch cubes.

Remove shrimp from marinade, letting excess drip off (discard marinade). Grill shrimp over high heat, turning once, until cooked through, about 1 minute per side. Toss shrimp with remaining ⅓ cup marinade.

Toss lettuce, baguette cubes, and avocado with Caesar dressing. Top with shrimp. Sprinkle with cheese and serve.

Sea Scallops over Shallot-Herb Pasta

SERVES 4

Scallops and fennel, a somewhat refined duo, take on a casual air when tossed with herbed pasta. Choose larger scallops when possible, which are easier to handle on the grill. Tongs can tear the delicate meat; instead, use a metal spatula to turn them, or thread onto skewers. For othe fennel, if you don't have a grill basket, halve the fennel bulb lengthwise and cut it into wedges, keeping the root intact so it holds together when grilling.

Coarse salt and freshly ground pepper

¾ pound spaghetti or linguine

3 shallots, minced (about ¼ cup)

½ cup plus 1½ teaspoons extra-virgin olive oil, plus more for grill

1 tablespoon fresh lemon juice

2 cups mixed fresh herbs, such as mint, flat-leaf parsley, tarragon, and basil, finely chopped

1 fennel bulb, trimmed, halved lengthwise, and thinly sliced crosswise, plus ¼ cup snipped fronds

24 sea scallops (about 1¼ pounds), tough muscle removed

Bring a large pot of salted water to a boil over high heat. Add pasta and cook until al dente according to package instructions.

Meanwhile, place minced shallots on a cutting board and sprinkle with 1 teaspoon salt. Using the side of a knife, crush into a paste. Transfer to a medium bowl, and whisk in 6 tablespoons oil and the lemon juice. Add herbs and fennel fronds, and mix well. Season with salt and pepper.

Drain pasta in a colander and return to pot. Stir in herb sauce. Cover to keep warm.

Heat grill to medium-high. Toss fennel slices with 1½ teaspoons oil, and season with salt and pepper. Toss scallops with remaining 2 tablespoons oil. Season with salt and pepper. Thread onto skewers (soaked for 30 minutes if wooden), if using.

Lightly oil grates. Using a grill basket, grill fennel until just wilted and starting to brown, about 5 minutes. Grill scallops, turning halfway through, until golden and just cooked through, 2 to 3 minutes total. Serve scallops and fennel over pasta.

TIP: When cleaning scallops, check to make sure the small, tough side muscle, called the adductor, has been removed by the fishmonger. If not, pinch the tough tissue on the side of the scallop between your fingers and pull it away.

Whole Fish with Potatoes, Chiles, and Fennel

SERVES 6

A platter of herbed, whole striped bass, fiery chiles, caramelized fennel, and grilled potatoes is not only one of the most satisfying combinations for fish lovers, it's also one of the most deliciously fragrant. If the heat of habaneros is too intense, you can opt for milder chiles of your choice.

3 fennel bulbs, trimmed and cut into 1-inch wedges, plus fronds

½ cup fresh flat-leaf parsley leaves

2 teaspoons black peppercorns

2 teaspoons pink peppercorns

4 garlic cloves

¼ cup plus 2 tablespoons extra-virgin olive oil, plus more for grill

1 whole striped bass or snapper (3¾ to 4 pounds), cleaned, head and tail left intact

2 cups mixed herb sprigs, such as mint, oregano, and flat-leaf parsley

2 pounds small potatoes, scrubbed

Coarse salt and freshly ground pepper

12 habanero or other chiles

2 teaspoons fresh oregano leaves

Mixed Herb Sauce (page 109), for serving

Using a mortar and pestle, crush ½ cup fennel fronds, parsley, peppercorns, and garlic to a coarse paste. (Or pulse in a food processor.) Stir in 2 tablespoons oil. Rub mixture over fish, inside and out; stuff fish with remaining fennel fronds and the herb sprigs. Cover with plastic wrap and let stand 30 minutes.

Cover potatoes by 2 inches of water in a medium saucepan; add 1 tablespoon salt. Bring to a boil, reduce to a simmer, and cook until just tender, 15 to 20 minutes; drain. Let cool slightly and halve.

Heat grill to medium. Season fish generously with salt and pepper. Using an oiled grill basket, grill fish, covered, turning once, until opaque and flesh flakes when tested with the tip of a knife, 20 to 25 minutes.

Meanwhile, toss fennel wedges, chiles, and potatoes with ¼ cup oil and season with salt. Grill vegetables, turning occasionally, until lightly marked and tender, 5 to 8 minutes. Toss potatoes with oregano and season with salt.

Arrange fish on a platter; surround with potatoes, fennel, and chiles. Drizzle with herb sauce and serve.

Grilled Halloumi Cheese and Vegetables with Smoky-Tomato Dressing

SERVES 4

Halloumi cheese, a lightly salted Greek specialty made from sheep's and goat's milk, can handle the high heat of the grill, softening without melting. It's a "meaty" cheese that's substantial enough to be the centerpiece of this platter of grilled mushrooms, fennel, red onion, and radicchio. Once they're all together on a platter, everything is dressed with a smoky relish and topped with fresh mint.

3 tomatoes (about 1 pound), halved crosswise

⅓ cup extra-virgin olive oil, plus more for grill and brushing

Coarse salt and freshly ground pepper

3 tablespoons red-wine vinegar

¾ cup fresh mint leaves, plus more for serving

1 small red onion, cut into 1-inch-thick wedges, root end intact

1 head radicchio, cut into wedges, root end intact

4 portobello mushrooms, trimmed and halved

4 ounces oyster mushrooms

2 fennel bulbs, trimmed and quartered lengthwise

8 ounces halloumi cheese, cut into pieces

Heat grill to medium-high. Brush tomatoes with oil; season with salt and pepper. Lightly oil grates. Grill tomatoes, cut-side down, until charred and beginning to soften, 3 to 4 minutes. Finely chop and transfer to a medium bowl. Stir in oil, vinegar, and mint; season with salt and pepper.

Brush onion, radicchio, mushrooms, and fennel with oil; season with salt and pepper. Grill until tender and charred in spots, 6 to 8 minutes. Brush halloumi with oil. Grill, turning once, until softened and golden, about 2 minutes on the first side and 1 minute on the second side.

Transfer vegetables and cheese to a platter. Drizzle with dressing, top with mint leaves, and serve with extra dressing on the side.

Soba Salad with Grilled Eggplant and Tomato

SERVES 4

Grilling can transform the taste of vegetables like eggplant and tomatoes, making them meltingly tender. Here they combine with toasted sesame oil, soy sauce, and lemon juice to create an irresistible sauce for soba noodles. The noodles are delicious at room temperature and often served cold, as well, making this a meal that you can have ready and waiting when your guests arrive.

1 medium eggplant, cut lengthwise into 1-inch slices

Coarse salt

1 medium tomato, halved

2 tablespoons vegetable oil, plus more for grill and brushing

8 ounces soba noodles

3 scallions, thinly sliced diagonally

¼ cup soy sauce

Juice of 1 to 2 lemons (about ¼ cup)

2 teaspoons toasted sesame oil

Fresh cilantro leaves, chopped, for serving

In a medium bowl, sprinkle eggplant slices generously with salt. Let stand 30 minutes, then rinse and pat dry.

Heat grill to medium-high. Liberally brush cut sides of eggplant and both sides of tomato with vegetable oil. Lightly oil grates. Grill vegetables, turning occasionally, until tender, about 4 minutes per side. Transfer to a cutting board. When cool enough to handle, cut into 1-inch pieces.

Bring a large pot of salted water to a boil. Cook soba until al dente, according to package instructions. Drain, then run under cold water. Shake dry.

Toss noodles with scallions, soy sauce, lemon juice, vegetable oil, and sesame oil in a medium bowl. Add eggplant and tomato, and season with salt. Serve at room temperature, or refrigerate 1 to 2 hours to serve chilled. Toss before serving and top with cilantro.

On the Side

That gloriously grilled centerpiece deserves an equally impressive mate. Whether for a backyard supper or a potluck barbecue, you want to contribute a side that stands out from the crowd. Our solution: Take a timeless salad of raw or grilled vegetables or grains and give it a bit of a twist. Potato salad gets lively with crisp green beans, whole-grain mustard, olive oil, and herbs. A rustic panzanella is made not with the usual tomatoes but with ripe, juicy peaches. The grill brings out wonderful smoky notes in corn for a salad with scallion and mint, and lifts the flavor of kale and radicchio with just a light char. Grilled or raw, these sides bring fresh flavors to any meal.

Watermelon, Orange, and Feta Salad

SERVES 4

Mildly sweet and refreshing fruits such as watermelon and orange
really take to the salty tang of feta. We chose to dress the salad
modestly—with a drizzle of olive oil and a generous sprinkling of salt
and pepper—to keep the focus on the main players.

¼ small red onion, very thinly sliced

¼ small (6-pound) seedless watermelon,
rind removed, flesh cut into ¼-inch
slices

1 large orange, peel and pith removed,
flesh cut into segments

2 ounces feta cheese, sliced or crumbled

¼ cup fresh flat-leaf parsley leaves

4 teaspoons extra-virgin olive oil

Coarse salt and freshly ground pepper

Place onion in a small bowl of ice water. Let
stand 10 minutes, then drain and pat dry.

Arrange watermelon, orange segments,
onion, feta, and parsley on a serving platter.
Drizzle with oil, and season with salt and
pepper.

Potato and Green Bean Salad

SERVES 4

Whether it's classic or contemporary, French- or German-style potato salad is welcome at just about every casual barbecue and grilled dinner. This one gets a crunch from gently simmered fresh green beans and a tangy bite from whole-grain mustard. The best potatoes to use are small red, white, or yellow waxy varieties, which hold their shape and retain their flavor after boiling. Cook the beans and potatoes separately but in the same saucepan, so you only need to boil one pot of water.

½ **medium red onion, thinly sliced**

Coarse salt

6 **ounces green beans, trimmed**

2 **pounds small potatoes, peeled**

¼ **cup extra-virgin olive oil**

4 **teaspoons fresh lemon juice (from 1 lemon)**

4 **teaspoons whole-grain mustard**

2 **teaspoons chopped fresh thyme leaves**

Place onion in a small bowl of ice water. Let stand 10 minutes, then drain and pat dry.

Meanwhile, bring a large pot of salted water to a boil. Add green beans, reduce to a simmer, and cook until just tender and bright green, 2 to 3 minutes. Using a slotted spoon or wire-mesh skimmer, transfer to a bowl of ice water. Drain green beans and pat dry. Add potatoes to same pot and simmer until tender, 10 to 15 minutes. Drain potatoes and halve them.

Whisk together oil, lemon juice, mustard, and thyme in a large bowl. Add potatoes and onion. Gently toss to combine. Season with salt. If not serving immediately, refrigerate, covered, up to overnight. Toss in beans just before serving.

Grilled Kale and Radicchio with Balsamic-Orange Glaze

SERVES 6 TO 8

Simmering balsamic vinegar with orange juice and zest results in a syrupy base for a dressing that brings out the best in grilled kale and radicchio. Both leafy vegetables become tender under high heat, and the grill softens any inherent bitterness. Make sure to turn the radicchio and kale as they cook—you're looking for a few charred spots to impart smokiness, while retaining those signature green and purple hues.

⅓ cup balsamic vinegar

2 large strips of orange zest plus ¼ cup fresh juice (from 1 orange)

¼ cup plus 2 tablespoons extra-virgin olive oil, plus more for grill

1½ pounds lacinato kale (3 to 4 bunches), thickest stems trimmed

2 heads radicchio, each cut into 6 wedges, core left intact

Coarse salt and freshly ground pepper

⅓ cup whole almonds, toasted and coarsely chopped

Bring vinegar and orange zest and juice to a rapid simmer in a small saucepan over medium-high heat, and cook until reduced to ¼ cup, about 5 minutes. Let cool slightly (discard zest). Whisk in 2 tablespoons oil.

Heat grill to medium. Toss kale and radicchio with remaining ¼ cup oil and 2 teaspoons salt; season with pepper. Lightly oil grates. Separate out radicchio, and grill, turning occasionally, until tender and lightly charred in places, 8 to 10 minutes. Transfer to a large bowl and toss while still warm with 1 tablespoon dressing.

Working in batches, grill kale, turning frequently, until wilted, about 6 minutes per batch; transfer to bowl with radicchio, and toss while still warm with 1 tablespoon dressing. Add almonds and remaining dressing until thoroughly coated. Serve on a large platter.

TIP: For perfectly toasted almonds, spread nuts evenly on a baking sheet and toast in a 350°F oven, stirring occasionally, until lightly golden, about 10 minutes.

Peach Panzanella

SERVES 6 TO 8

A quick ingredient swap is all it takes to reimagine panzanella. This rustic Italian salad usually features tomatoes and cubes of day-old Tuscan-style bread (made without salt), soaked in a basic vinaigrette and tossed with fresh basil and perhaps other vegetables. Here, slices of ripe, juicy peaches in place of the tomatoes bring a different and welcome sweetness to the mix.

2 pounds ripe peaches, pitted and sliced

1 medium red onion, thinly sliced

1 garlic clove, lightly smashed

5 tablespoons extra-virgin olive oil, plus more for grill

3 tablespoons red-wine vinegar

Coarse salt and freshly ground pepper

5 slices (each 1 inch thick) day-old Tuscan-style bread

4 Kirby cucumbers (about 12 ounces), peeled and sliced

1 cup fresh basil leaves

Place peaches, onion, and garlic in a large nonreactive bowl. Drizzle oil and vinegar over peach mixture. Season with salt and pepper, and toss to combine. Let stand, covered, in a cool place, at least 1 hour or up to 4 hours.

Heat grill to medium-high. Lightly oil grates. Grill bread, turning once, until crisp and grill marks appear, 2 to 3 minutes. Remove from heat and rub lightly with garlic (from marinade), if desired. Tear bread into bite-size chunks.

Before serving, add cucumbers, basil, and bread to peach mixture. Toss to coat bread thoroughly. Season with salt and pepper, and remove garlic clove before serving.

Grilled Corn, Mint, and Scallion Salad

SERVES 6 TO 8

When sweet corn is in season, it's high time for eating it straight from the cob. But for something a little special, toss together this salad: The mint and scallion heighten the flavors. For easy cleanup, work on a rimmed baking sheet when slicing corn from the cob to contain the kernels.

10 ears corn, shucked

3 bunches scallions, trimmed

Extra-virgin olive oil, for grill and brushing

Coarse salt and freshly ground pepper

⅔ cup fresh mint leaves, torn if large

Heat grill to high. Brush corn and scallions with oil; season with salt and pepper. Lightly oil grates. Grill corn, turning occasionally, until lightly charred and tender, 6 to 8 minutes. Let cool, then cut kernels off cobs (about 5 cups).

Meanwhile, grill scallions until charred, about 2 minutes. Cut into 1-inch pieces.

Toss corn, scallions, and mint together in a large serving bowl. Season with salt and pepper.

Baby Bok Choy Slaw

SERVES 8

This slaw, made from small heads of bok choy, demonstrates that you don't need a lot of ingredients to make an impact. Tossed with fresh chiles and a light sesame dressing, it pairs nicely with burgers, chicken, and fish. If you're making the slaw more than an hour in advance, store it in the refrigerator, then let it stand at room temperature for about 30 minutes; drain off any accumulated liquid before serving.

3 **pounds baby bok choy, trimmed and thinly sliced lengthwise**

⅓ **cup unseasoned rice vinegar**

1 **tablespoon toasted sesame oil**

1 **tablespoon vegetable oil**

2 **chiles, such as Fresno or serrano, and seeded, if desired, thinly sliced into rounds**

Coarse salt

Toss together bok choy, vinegar, both oils, and chiles in a large bowl. Season with salt. Let stand until bok choy collapses to half its volume (it will darken slightly), 20 to 30 minutes. Toss again before serving.

Cabbage and Radish Slaw with Peanut Dressing

SERVES 8 TO 10

Mild white daikon is a cousin of the red radish, which has a sharper bite. This slaw features both, along with a peanut dressing that can be made up to four days ahead. You can let this slaw stand up to one hour after dressing it; if you do so, stir in the peanuts and red radishes just before serving so they stay crunchy.

1 tablespoon finely chopped peeled fresh ginger

¼ cup coarsely chopped shallot

¼ cup plus 1 tablespoon creamy peanut butter

½ cup unseasoned rice vinegar

3 tablespoons soy sauce

3 tablespoons dark-brown sugar

¼ cup vegetable oil

1 small green cabbage (about 1¾ pounds), finely shredded

1 medium daikon radish, cut into ⅛-inch-thick matchsticks

16 red radishes, halved lengthwise and cut into thin half-moons

4 scallions, cut on the diagonal into long, thin slices

½ cup roasted unsalted peanuts

Blend ginger, shallot, peanut butter, vinegar, soy sauce, sugar, and oil in a blender until smooth.

Place cabbage, radishes, scallions, and peanuts in a large serving bowl. Add peanut dressing and toss thoroughly to combine.

Baby Bok Choy Slaw

Cabbage and Radish Slaw with Peanut Dressing

Farro with Zucchini, Pine Nuts, and Lemon Zest

SERVES 8 TO 10

Farro is a type of hulled wheat that has been cultivated in Italy for centuries. The chewy, nutty grain gives soups and salads heft and texture, and is substantial enough to turn a salad like this into a vegetarian main dish. Choose whole farro instead of semi-pearled (part of the bran is removed) or pearled (all of the bran is removed)—more of its nutrients are left intact. Barley and bulgur wheat are good alternatives to farro.

¾ pound farro (about 1¾ cups)

Coarse salt and freshly ground pepper

1 small shallot, finely chopped

Zest and juice of 1 to 2 lemons, to taste

3 tablespoons extra-virgin olive oil

½ cup pine nuts

1 pound zucchini, thinly sliced crosswise

½ cup fresh flat-leaf parsley leaves, coarsely chopped

4 ounces Parmigiano-Reggiano cheese, shaved

Place farro in a large saucepan with enough cold water to cover by about 3 inches. Bring to a boil over high heat; season with 1 tablespoon salt. Reduce heat to medium and simmer until farro is al dente according to package instructions; drain and let cool.

Combine shallot with lemon juice and salt to taste in a small bowl; let stand 15 minutes.

Meanwhile, heat oil in a small skillet over medium. Add pine nuts and cook, stirring frequently, until lightly toasted, about 5 minutes. Remove from heat and add lemon zest.

Place farro, pine-nut mixture, zucchini, and parsley in a large bowl, and stir to combine. Stir in shallot mixture. Season with salt and pepper.

Add half the cheese and toss to combine. (Salad can be refrigerated, covered, up to 6 hours.) Before serving, top with remaining cheese.

Sardinian Tomato Salad

SERVES 6 TO 8

We used a selection of deliciously ripe green and yellow heirloom tomatoes for this salad; feel free to substitute any variety to make the most of the season. (Just be sure not to use unripe green tomatoes, which are best for frying or pickling.) If you're grilling, toast up some bread—drizzled with oil and rubbed with garlic—to serve alongside the salad.

½ medium red onion, thinly sliced

½ teaspoon orange zest plus 2 tablespoons fresh juice

2 tablespoons champagne or white wine vinegar

¼ cup extra-virgin olive oil, plus more for drizzling

Coarse salt and freshly ground pepper

2¼ pounds small to medium ripe heirloom tomatoes, such as Green Zebra and Green Grape, cut into wedges

1 small fennel bulb, trimmed, halved, and thinly sliced lengthwise

½ cup mild green olives, such as Castelvetrano, smashed and pitted

1 tablespoon coarsely chopped fresh flat-leaf parsley leaves

Flaky sea salt, such as Maldon, for serving

Place onion in a small bowl of ice water. Let stand 10 minutes, then drain and pat dry.

Meanwhile, whisk together orange zest and juice and vinegar. Whisk in oil until emulsified. Season with 1 teaspoon coarse salt and ¼ teaspoon pepper.

In a large bowl, toss tomatoes, sliced fennel, olives, and onions with vinaigrette. Let stand at least 15 minutes or up to 2 hours.

Before serving, fold in parsley. Season with salt and pepper. Using a slotted spoon, transfer salad to a serving plate or bowl. Spoon some juices from bottom of large bowl over top. Pour remaining juices into a small serving bowl or pitcher and serve alongside. Sprinkle salad with flaky salt and fennel fronds, and drizzle with oil.

Grilled Ratatouille and Bulgur Salad

SERVES 4

All the components of the quintessential Provençal vegetable dish are united at the grill, giving them a smoky undertone. Tomatoes and zucchini release their juices when cooked on the stove; on the grill, these vegetables caramelize, resulting in a concentrated version of the stew. Ratatouille also makes terrific leftovers—you can eat it for days on end, with a fried egg and grilled bread.

1 cup bulgur, farro, or couscous

Coarse salt and freshly ground pepper

Extra-virgin olive oil

1 medium eggplant, cut lengthwise into ¾-inch-thick strips

1 medium zucchini, cut lengthwise into ¾-inch-thick strips

1 medium yellow summer squash, cut lengthwise into ¾-inch-thick strips

1 large onion, sliced into ¼-inch rounds

2 medium tomatoes, halved crosswise

2 tablespoons fresh lemon juice (from 1 lemon)

½ cup fresh basil leaves

Combine bulgur, 1½ cups water, a pinch of salt, and a drizzle of oil in a saucepan. Bring to a simmer, then cover and cook over low heat until tender, about 12 minutes. Remove from heat; let stand, covered, 10 minutes. Fluff with a fork.

Heat grill to medium-high. Brush eggplant, zucchini, squash, onion, and tomatoes with oil. Season with salt and pepper. Lightly oil grates. Grill vegetables, turning once, until lightly charred and tender, 5 to 8 minutes.

Transfer vegetables to a cutting board and chop into 1-inch pieces; reserve accumulated vegetable juices.

In a large bowl, toss bulgur with reserved vegetable juices. Add lemon juice, season with salt and pepper, and toss to combine. (Bulgur can be refrigerated in an airtight container up to 2 days; let come to room temperature before serving.)

Serve bulgur topped with chopped vegetables, basil, and a drizzle of oil.

Grilled Romaine and Radicchio with Polenta Croutons

SERVES 4

A lovely side, this grilled salad could also play a central role in a meatless meal. Sturdy lettuces like romaine and radicchio can stand up to high heat and serve as the salad base, with grilled polenta croutons adding substance. It's the perfect dish when you're hosting people with a variety of dietary preferences, as polenta is vegan.

2 teaspoons whole-grain mustard

2 tablespoons red-wine vinegar

¼ cup finely chopped shallot

¼ cup extra-virgin olive oil, plus more for grill and brushing

Coarse salt and freshly ground pepper

1 log (18 ounces) prepared polenta

1 head romaine, halved

1 head radicchio, quartered

Whisk together mustard, vinegar, shallot, and oil in a small bowl. Season with salt and pepper.

Heat grill to high. Slice polenta lengthwise into thirds, brush with oil, and season with salt and pepper. Lightly oil grates. Grill polenta until lightly charred and it can be turned without sticking to the grill, about 2 minutes per side. Remove from grill and cut into croutons.

Brush romaine and radicchio with oil, and season with salt and pepper. Grill lettuces, cut-side down, until slightly wilted and charred, about 1 minute. Arrange romaine, radicchio, and croutons on a platter, and drizzle with vinaigrette.

At the End

Whether you grill it or chill it, dessert is another opportunity to highlight seasonal produce (think berry-fizz floats and fruit cream pies), or to simply end the meal on a special note (who can resist a brownie sundae ice-cream cake?). Here, you'll find a roundup of our best-loved summer favorites: Take advantage of that still-warm grill to heat up a rich pound cake and top it with bourbon-splashed berries; or to grill your favorite stone fruit, then fold it into a creamy fool, fragrant with cardamom and spiced nuts. If you're planning ahead, prepare frozen treats, like Dark-Chocolate Ice Pops and Watermelon-Campari Granita. When you want to keep things short and deliciously sweet, a bowl of ice cream topped with a homemade sauce is about as easy (and satisfying) as dessert gets.

Iced Cocoa Pops

EACH MAKES 14 POPS

For this frozen dessert, we turned hot cocoa on its head to create two dreamy pops—one rich and dark, the other light and creamy. Our hot-cocoa pop contains only bittersweet chocolate, milk, cream, sugar, and a hint of nutmeg. A coconut milk variation offers a tropical pairing with white chocolate, while rum gives the icy pop a shot of warmth.

Dark-Chocolate Ice Pops

- 2 cups whole milk
- 1 cup heavy cream
- 5 ounces bittersweet chocolate (preferably at least 70% cacao), chopped (about 1 cup)
- 2 tablespoons light-brown sugar
- ¼ teaspoon freshly grated nutmeg

Warm milk and cream in a medium saucepan over medium-low heat. Add chocolate, and whisk until melted and combined. Add sugar and whisk until dissolved. Continue to warm mixture until thickened, about 5 minutes. Whisk in nutmeg. Let cool slightly.

Divide mixture evenly among fourteen 2½-ounce ice-pop molds. Seal with tops, insert sticks (if you're not using molds with reusable sticks), and freeze until set, at least 6 hours (preferably overnight). Remove pops from molds. Serve immediately.

White-Chocolate Ice Pops

- 1 cup whole milk
- 1 cup unsweetened coconut milk
- 1 cup heavy cream
- 5 ounces white chocolate, chopped (about 1 cup)
- 1 tablespoon rum

Warm whole milk, coconut milk, and cream in a medium saucepan over medium-low heat. Add chocolate, and whisk until melted and combined. Continue to warm mixture until thickened, about 5 minutes. Whisk in rum. Let cool sightly.

Divide mixture evenly among fourteen 2½-ounce ice-pop molds. Seal with tops, insert sticks (if you're not using molds with reusable sticks), and freeze until set, at least 6 hours (preferably overnight). Remove pops from molds. Serve immediately.

TIP: To loosen an ice pop before serving, briefly dip the mold into warm water.

Berry Fizz Float

MAKES 4 TO 6 FLOATS

With twists like this, you can see why the classic ice cream float—
that old-fashioned favorite—will never go out of style. Macerated
berries add sweet layers to vanilla ice cream (or any flavor you please),
and seltzer offers effervescence. You can also serve the berries as a
topping for pancakes or shortcake.

4 cups mixed berries, such as
raspberries, blueberries, and
strawberries, larger berries halved

½ cup sugar

Ice cream

Seltzer

Combine berries with sugar and let stand, stirring occasionally, until berries release liquid, about 45 minutes. In a large glass, alternate scoops of berries with scoops of ice cream, and top it all off with seltzer. Serve immediately with a straw and spoon and repeat with the remaining ingredients.

Peach Sherbet and Sorbet

EACH SERVES 6

Here's an ingenious way to enjoy a frozen treat without an ice cream maker: To make sherbet, blend frozen fresh peaches with sweetened condensed milk. For sorbet, use just sugar, lemon juice, and salt with the fruit. The frosty results make for a true taste of summer. You can blend the desserts on the spot, or make them up to three days ahead.

Peach Sherbet

- 6 large ripe peaches, peeled and sliced, and frozen until firm
- 1 cup sweetened condensed milk

Using a food processor or blender, blend peaches with condensed milk until creamy and smooth. Eat immediately, soft-serve-style, or freeze in a loaf pan and store, covered, up to 3 days.

Peach Sorbet

- 6 large ripe peaches, peeled and sliced, and frozen until firm
- ¾ cup sugar
- 1 teaspoon fresh lemon juice (from 1 lemon)

  Coarse salt

Using a food processor or blender, blend peaches with sugar, lemon juice, and a pinch of salt until smooth and creamy. Eat immediately, soft-serve-style, or freeze in a loaf pan, scraping occasionally, and store, covered, up to 3 days.

Brownie Sundae Ice-Cream Cake

SERVES 10

Once assembled and chilled, this frozen dessert becomes a sliceable sundae that shows off every layer. Measure your loaf pan at increments to ensure a perfect fit, and use an offset spatula to spread the fillings—peanut butter, ice cream, berries—to the edges of the pan. Top everything off with whipped cream, candied nuts, and gourmet cherries, and watch it disappear.

FOR THE CAKE

Vegetable-oil cooking spray, for pan

⅔ cup all-purpose flour

¼ cup Dutch-process cocoa powder

Coarse salt

½ teaspoon baking powder

½ cup (1 stick) unsalted butter, room temperature

1 cup sugar

2 large eggs, room temperature

1 teaspoon pure vanilla extract

⅓ cup whole milk

4 ounces bittersweet chocolate (preferably 70% cacao), melted

FOR THE ASSEMBLY

½ cup crunchy peanut butter

1¼ cups vanilla ice cream, softened

½ cup crushed raspberries

1½ cups strawberry ice cream, softened

Lightly Sweetened Whipped Cream and Sugared Peanuts (recipes follow)

Maraschino cherries (preferably Luxardo), for serving

Make the cake: Preheat oven to 375°F. Coat a 9-by-13-inch baking pan with cooking spray. Line with parchment, leaving a 2-inch overhang on long sides; coat parchment with cooking spray. Whisk together flour, cocoa, ¾ teaspoon salt, and the baking powder in a medium bowl.

In a large bowl, using a mixer on medium speed, beat butter with sugar until pale and fluffy, about 3 minutes. Add eggs, one at a time, beating until smooth. Beat in vanilla extract. With mixer on low speed, add flour mixture in 3 batches, alternating with milk in 2 batches, beating until combined. Beat in melted chocolate.

Transfer batter to prepared pan, smoothing top with an offset spatula. Bake until set on top but still wobbly in center, about 15 minutes. Let cool completely in pan on a wire rack.

To assemble: Line a 4½-by-8½-inch loaf pan with plastic wrap. Use parchment to lift cake from baking pan. Cut crosswise into 3 pieces, with 1 piece cut to fit bottom of loaf pan exactly, the next slightly wider, and the last widest of all (to match size of pan, which gets wider toward top).

Place smallest cake piece, top-side up, in bottom of lined loaf pan. Using an offset spatula, spread peanut butter over top, then vanilla ice cream. Place second-largest cake piece, top-side down, on ice cream. Spread with raspberries, then strawberry ice cream.

Top with final cake piece, top-side down. Cover with plastic wrap and freeze until firm, at least 6 hours and up to 24 hours.

Run a butter knife around edges to release lined cake from pan, then use plastic wrap to remove cake and place on a serving platter. Top with whipped cream and sprinkle with peanuts. Slice with a serrated knife, wiping blade clean between each cut. Transfer slices to chilled plates using a cake server or metal spatula, and serve with cherries and more peanuts.

Lightly Sweetened Whipped Cream

MAKES ABOUT 2 CUPS

- 1 cup cold heavy cream
- 2 tablespoons confectioners' sugar

Using a mixer or by hand, whisk cream in a well-chilled bowl until soft peaks form. Add sugar, as desired (or omit, for unsweetened whipped cream), and whisk until medium-stiff peaks form.

Sugared Peanuts

MAKES ABOUT 2 CUPS

- ½ cup sugar
- 1¼ cups roasted salted peanuts
- Coarse salt

Bring sugar and 2 tablespoons water to a boil in a medium saucepan, stirring until sugar is dissolved. Continue to cook, until a candy thermometer inserted in mixture registers 235°F.

Add peanuts and stir until sugar begins to crystallize and form a sandy coating, about 1 minute. Stir in ½ teaspoon salt and cook, stirring, until nuts darken slightly, about 3 minutes more. Pour in a single layer onto a parchment-lined rimmed baking sheet and let cool completely before serving. (Sugared peanuts can be stored in an airtight container at room temperature up to 1 week.)

Sundae Sauces

With a variety of toppings, it's easy to turn plain scoops of ice cream into delightful desserts for a summer dinner party, an afternoon barbecue, or a lazy-day treat. These can all be refrigerated up to one week—if they last that long.

Lime Curd

MAKES 2 CUPS

- 2 large eggs, plus 6 large yolks
- 1 cup sugar
- 4 teaspoons lime zest plus juice of 6 limes (about ¾ cup)
- 6 tablespoons unsalted butter, room temperature
- Coarse salt

Whisk together eggs, yolks, sugar, zest and juice, butter, and 1¼ teaspoons salt in a saucepan. Bring to a simmer over medium-low heat, whisking constantly; cook until thickened, about 5 minutes. Strain through a fine-mesh sieve into a bowl (discard solids). Press plastic wrap directly onto surface of curd. Refrigerate at least 1 hour and up to 24 hours.

Vanilla-Bourbon Butterscotch

MAKES 1 CUP

- 1 cup packed light-brown sugar
- ½ cup (1 stick) unsalted butter
- 1 vanilla bean, split lengthwise
- ⅓ cup heavy cream
- 1 to 2 tablespoons bourbon
- Coarse salt

Bring sugar, butter, and vanilla to a boil. Cook, stirring occasionally, about 2 minutes. Remove from heat. Stir in cream, bourbon, and ¼ teaspoon salt. Bring to a boil and cook for about 30 seconds. Let cool slightly before serving.

Hot Fudge Sauce

MAKES 1½ CUPS

- 1 cup heavy cream
- ½ cup light corn syrup
- 12 ounces semisweet chocolate, finely chopped

Combine heavy cream and corn syrup in a saucepan over medium heat. Cook until bubbles appear. Remove from heat. Add chocolate and whisk until melted.

Fresh-Strawberry Sauce

MAKES 1½ CUPS

- 1 pound strawberries, quartered
- 1 cup plus 2 tablespoons sugar
- Coarse salt
- 1 tablespoon fresh lemon juice (from 1 lemon)

Stir together strawberries, sugar, ¼ teaspoon salt, and the lemon juice in a medium saucepan. Bring to a boil, mashing and stirring frequently. Cook at a low boil, stirring more frequently as mixture thickens, until sauce clings to a spoon, about 10 minutes. Skim foam from top. Let cool completely.

Lime Curd

Vanilla-Bourbon Butterscotch

Hot Fudge Sauce

Fresh-Strawberry Sauce

Grilled Pound Cake with Seasonal Fruit

SERVES 4

Buttery, grilled pound cake—especially topped with fruit that's been treated to a touch of bourbon—may have you rethinking fruit cobbler as your go-to treat. When your berries are exceptionally ripe and sweet, skip the first step and top with the unadulterated fresh fruit. If you're baking your own cake, make it ahead to allow it to cool completely before slicing and grilling.

3 tablespoons sugar

2 tablespoons bourbon

1 cup blueberries

1 cup strawberries, quartered

2 apricots, pits removed and flesh cut into wedges

1 cup raspberries

2 tablespoons unsalted butter, room temperature

4 (¾-inch) slices pound cake, homemade (page 247) or store-bought

Extra-virgin olive oil, for grill

Lightly Sweetened Whipped Cream (page 221) or crème fraîche, for serving

Fresh mint leaves, for serving

Heat grill to medium-high. In a large cast-iron skillet, combine sugar, bourbon, and 2 tablespoons water. Place skillet on grill and cook, stirring occasionally, until sugar dissolves. Add blueberries, strawberries, and apricots, and cook until fruit is warmed through, about 2 minutes. Remove from heat and stir in raspberries. Let stand 5 minutes.

Butter both sides of each cake slice. Lightly oil grates. Grill pound cake, turning quickly, until golden brown, about 10 seconds per side. Serve topped with fruit mixture, whipped cream, and mint.

Fruit Granitas

EACH SERVES 8 TO 10

Ice, sugar, and fruit combine to create these invigorating, no-frills granitas—no special equipment required. You can freeze the adults-only watermelon and mint-spiked lemon granitas for up to one month.

Watermelon Campari

- 1 (4-pound) wedge of watermelon, seeded, rind removed, flesh cut into 2-inch chunks
- ½ cup superfine sugar
  Juice of 2 limes (about ¼ cup)
- 2 tablespoons Campari

Arrange watermelon in a single layer on a parchment-lined rimmed baking sheet, or in a resealable plastic bag. Place in freezer until frozen, about 1½ hours. (Transfer watermelon to airtight freezer bags if not using immediately.)

Place frozen chunks in a food processor; process until smooth. Add sugar, lime juice, and Campari; process until fully incorporated, about 5 minutes, scraping down sides of food processor as necessary.

Transfer mixture to a 9-by-13-inch glass baking dish; place in freezer. Chill until mixture begins to solidify, about 45 minutes. Remove from freezer; stir with a fork until mixture begins to break up. Refreeze, scraping with fork every 30 minutes, until completely frozen and fine crystals form, about 2 hours total. Serve granita in chilled glasses or bowls.

Lemon and Mint

- 1 cup sugar
- 6 sprigs mint
  Zest and juice of 2 lemons (about ¼ cup)

Combine 3 cups water, the sugar, and mint in a medium pot. Heat over medium, stirring, until sugar dissolves, about 5 minutes. Place syrup in a medium bowl set over ice water. Remove mint. Add lemon zest and juice, and stir mixture until it is icy cold.

Transfer to a 9-by-13-inch glass baking dish; place in freezer. Chill until mixture begins to solidify, about 45 minutes. Remove from freezer; stir with a fork until mixture begins to break up. Refreeze, scraping with fork every 30 minutes, until completely frozen and fine crystals form, about 3 hours total. Serve granita in chilled glasses or bowls.

Grilled Stone-Fruit Fool

SERVES 6

Fruit fool, a traditional British dessert, involves folding pureed fruit into a custard or whipped cream, then spiking it with whole pieces of fruit or berries. It is simplicity itself. Our version boasts the more exotic orange-blossom water, available online and at some Middle Eastern grocers, together with cardamom. Grill your fruit before or after dinner (whenever your grill is free and still hot) and let it cool until you're ready to make dessert. Maximize the make-ahead aspect of this dessert by steeping the cream overnight, grilling the fruit up to two days ahead, and making the gingered nuts in advance.

8 cardamom pods

3 tablespoons sugar

1½ cups heavy cream

Extra-virgin olive oil, for grill

2 pounds ripe stone-fruit, such as pluots, apricots, or plums, halved and pitted

1 teaspoon orange-blossom water (optional)

½ cup Gingered Nuts (page 247)

Crush cardamom pods to release the seeds. Grind cardamom seeds and sugar together with a mortar and pestle or in a spice grinder, until sugar is lightly flecked with cardamom. Reserve 1 teaspoon sugar mixture and stir remaining mixture into cream. Cover and refrigerate until just before serving, up to 24 hours.

Heat grill to medium-low. Lightly oil grates. Lightly sprinkle fruit halves with reserved cardamom sugar. Grill, cut-side down, until lightly caramelized, 2 to 3 minutes. Turn gently and continue cooking until bubbling, about 10 minutes. Let cool. Remove skins, and puree or chop fruit.

Stir cream to dissolve sugar and add orange-blossom water, if desired. Whisk cream until soft peaks form. To serve, spoon whipped cream and fruit into individual glasses or bowls in alternating layers. Sprinkle with gingered nuts.

Summer-Fruit Cream Pie

SERVES 12

Farmstand berries get folded into cool custard for this fill-and-chill cream pie. A press-in graham cracker crust assures ease of assembly, letting you focus on the grilling at hand.

1 cup sugar

3 tablespoons plus 2 teaspoons cornstarch

¼ teaspoon salt

2¾ cups whole milk

4 large egg yolks

⅛ teaspoon ground cinnamon

4 tablespoons unsalted butter, room temperature

½ cup blueberries

½ cup raspberries

½ cup blackberries

Graham Cracker Crust (recipe follows)

1 cup Peaches in Syrup (recipe follows)

Whisk sugar, cornstarch, and salt together in a medium saucepan. Whisk in milk. Cook over medium-high heat, stirring constantly with a wooden spoon, until bubbling and thickened, about 7 minutes total (about 2 minutes after it comes to a boil).

Whisk yolks in a medium bowl until combined. Add milk mixture in a slow, steady stream, whisking until completely incorporated. Return mixture to saucepan, and cook over medium heat, stirring constantly and scraping sides, until it returns to a boil, 1 to 2 minutes. Remove from heat.

Stir in cinnamon and add butter 1 tablespoon at a time, whisking until butter melts before adding another piece. Let custard cool in saucepan on a wire rack, whisking occasionally, at least 10 minutes and up to 1 hour. Gently fold in berries until evenly distributed.

Pour custard into graham cracker crust. Press plastic wrap directly on surface of custard. Refrigerate until custard filling is chilled and firm, at least 4 hours or up to overnight. Spoon peaches with syrup onto pie and serve.

Graham Cracker Crust

MAKES ONE 9-INCH CRUST

- 1½ cups finely ground graham crackers (about 12 crackers)
- 6 tablespoons unsalted butter, melted
- ¼ cup sugar

  Coarse salt

Preheat oven to 350°F. Pulse graham cracker crumbs, butter, sugar, and ⅛ teaspoon salt in a food processor until combined.

Firmly press crumb mixture into bottom and up sides of a 9-inch pie dish. Bake until crust is fragrant and edges are golden, 12 to 14 minutes. Let cool completely on a wire rack.

Peaches in Syrup

MAKES 2 CUPS

- 1½ pounds (about 8 small) ripe peaches, bottoms scored with an X
- 1⅓ cups sugar
- 2 tablespoons fresh lemon juice (from 1 lemon)

  Coarse salt

Peel, halve, and pit peaches. Cut each half into 6 wedges.

Bring peaches along with accumulated juices, ½ cup water, the sugar, lemon juice, and a pinch of salt to a simmer in a medium saucepan over medium heat. Cook, stirring occasionally, until sugar dissolves, about 2 minutes. Transfer to a medium bowl. Let cool completely, cover, and refrigerate overnight.

Prepare an ice-water bath. Transfer peach mixture to a medium saucepan (reserve bowl), and bring to a boil. Skim foam from surface. Cook, stirring occasionally, until peaches are tender, 8 to 10 minutes. Return peach mixture to bowl. Let cool in ice-water bath. Use peaches immediately, or refrigerate in an airtight container up to 2 weeks.

Tahini Sauce

Tapenade

Chimichurri

Rouille

Sauces, Marinades, and More

The right sauce can turn a plain dish into something extraordinary. An herbed salsa verde or chimichurri brightens fish or steaks; creamy rouille and aïöli are lovely with vegetables, and yogurt-based sauces lend a cool touch to spicy foods. The essential recipes on these pages are truly versatile mixtures that you'll use again and again.

Tahini Sauce

MAKES 1¼ CUPS

- ½ cup tahini
- Zest and fresh juice of 1 lemon
- 1 tablespoon extra-virgin olive oil
- 1 garlic clove, chopped
- ½ teaspoon cumin
- ½ teaspoon paprika
- Coarse salt

In a food processor, puree tahini, lemon zest and juice, oil, garlic, cumin, paprika, and ¾ cup water until smooth. Season with salt. (Tahini sauce can be refrigerated in an airtight container up to 3 days.)

Tapenade

MAKES 1½ CUPS

- 2 teaspoons fresh thyme leaves, finely chopped
- 3 anchovy fillets, preferably packed in olive oil, finely chopped
- 2 tablespoons capers, preferably salt-packed, drained, rinsed, and coarsely chopped
- 1 garlic clove, minced
- 2 cups black olives, such as niçoise or Kalamata, drained, pitted, and finely chopped
- ¼ cup plus 2 tablespoons extra-virgin olive oil

Place all ingredients in a medium bowl and mix well to combine; or pulse to combine in a food processor. (Tapenade can be refrigerated in an airtight container up to 2 weeks.)

Chimichurri

MAKES 1½ CUPS

- ½ cup finely chopped red onion
- ½ cup chopped fresh flat-leaf parsley leaves
- ⅓ cup extra-virgin olive oil
- ¼ cup sherry vinegar
- 2 tablespoons chopped fresh oregano leaves
- 1 tablespoon minced garlic
- 2 teaspoons coarse salt
- ½ teaspoon red-pepper flakes

  Freshly ground black pepper to taste

Stir together all ingredients in a medium bowl until well combined. (Chimichurri can be refrigerated in an airtight container up to 2 days.)

Rouille

MAKES 1½ CUPS

- ¼ cup boiling water, plus up to 2 tablespoons more if needed
- 1½ teaspoons saffron threads, crushed
- 2 garlic cloves, chopped

  Coarse salt
- 1 cup torn soft white bread, crust removed
- 1 large egg yolk, room temperature
- 1½ cups extra-virgin olive oil
- ¼ teaspoon cayenne pepper
- ¼ teaspoon sweet paprika

In a medium bowl, pour boiling water over saffron and steep 15 minutes.

Add a pinch of salt to garlic. Mash into a paste using the flat side of a knife or a mortar and pestle.

Add bread to saffron water and press to absorb. Add egg yolk to bread mixture and stir to combine. Gradually add ¼ cup oil, drop by drop, stirring constantly, until smooth. Whisk in remaining 1¼ cups oil in a steady stream.

Stir in garlic paste, cayenne, and paprika, and season with salt. (Rouille can be refrigerated in an airtight container up to 2 days.)

Yogurt–Cucumber Sauce

MAKES ABOUT 2½ CUPS

- 2 cups plain whole-milk Greek yogurt
- 2 Persian cucumbers, halved lengthwise, cut into 1-inch pieces (about 1¼ cups)
  Coarse salt
  Za'atar, for serving

Puree yogurt, cucumbers, and 1 teaspoon salt in a blender until smooth. Refrigerate, covered, at least 1 hour and up to 3 days. Generously sprinkle with za'atar just before serving.

Chopped–Chile Relish

MAKES ABOUT 1½ CUPS

- 8 ounces mild chiles, such as Anaheim or banana, or spicy chiles, such as Fresno or jalapeño, finely chopped
- ¼ cup extra-virgin olive oil
- 3 tablespoons red-wine vinegar
  Coarse salt

Stir together chiles, oil, vinegar, and ¼ teaspoon salt in a medium bowl. Let stand at room temperature at least 1 hour, or refrigerate, covered, up to 3 days. Bring to room temperature before serving.

Lebanese Tomato Sauce

MAKES ABOUT 1¾ CUPS

- 4 medium (about 1½ pounds) yellow, orange, or red tomatoes
- 2 tablespoons extra-virgin olive oil
- ¾ teaspoon cumin seeds, toasted
- ¼ teaspoon red-pepper flakes
  Coarse salt
- 3 garlic cloves, smashed

To peel the tomatoes, bring a pot of water to a boil. Prepare a large ice-water bath. Cut a shallow X in the bottom of each tomato, then place in pot and blanch 20 seconds. Use a slotted spoon to transfer tomatoes to ice bath just until cool, about 2 minutes. Remove and peel away skins; discard.

Core, halve, and squeeze tomatoes to remove seeds and pulp; discard. Transfer flesh to a food processor. Add oil, cumin, red-pepper flakes, and 1 teaspoon salt. Pulse just until a chunky sauce forms. Transfer to a medium bowl and stir in garlic. Refrigerate, covered, at least 8 hours and up to 3 days. Bring to room temperature and remove smashed garlic cloves before serving.

Aïoli

Salsa Verde

Romesco

Aïoli

MAKES 1½ CUPS

Coarse salt

2   garlic cloves, chopped

2   large egg yolks, room temperature

1   tablespoon fresh lemon juice

1¾   cups extra-virgin olive oil

Add a pinch of salt to garlic. Mash into a paste using the flat side of a knife or a mortar and pestle.

Whisk together egg yolks and ½ teaspoon salt in a medium bowl. Gradually add lemon juice and 1 tablespoon water in a slow steady stream, whisking until thoroughly blended. Add about ¼ cup oil, drop by drop, whisking until emulsified.

Gently whisk in 1¼ cups oil in a steady stream. Stir in garlic paste. (Aïoli can be refrigerated in an airtight container up to 2 days. If aïoli separates, whisk 1 egg yolk with 1 tablespoon tepid water in a medium bowl. Gradually whisk into aïoli until combined, then whisk in ¼ cup oil.)

Salsa Verde

MAKES ABOUT 1 CUP

1   teaspoon lemon zest plus 2 tablespoons fresh juice

1   teaspoon coarse salt

2   cups fresh flat-leaf parsley leaves, finely chopped

1   cup fresh mint leaves, finely chopped

1   tablespoon snipped fresh chives

½   cup extra-virgin olive oil

Stir together all ingredients until well combined. (Salsa verde can be refrigerated in an airtight container up to 2 days.)

Romesco

MAKES 1½ CUPS

½   cup plus 2 tablespoons extra-virgin olive oil, plus more for grill

2   red bell peppers

1   small garlic clove, smashed

½   cup raw almonds, toasted

1   tablespoon sherry vinegar

1   teaspoon pimentón (smoked paprika)

Coarse salt

Heat grill to high. Lightly oil grates. Grill peppers, turning occasionally, until skins are charred in spots, 15 to 18 minutes. Transfer peppers to a medium bowl, cover with a plate, and let steam 15 minutes. Remove charred skins and discard. Halve peppers, and discard seeds and stems.

Transfer peppers to a food processor. Add garlic, almonds, vinegar, and pimentón. Pulse until just combined into a thick, coarsely chopped sauce. With machine running, slowly add oil, processing until combined. Season with salt. (Romesco can be refrigerated in an airtight container up to 3 days; serve at room temperature.)

Almond Aïoli

MAKES ABOUT 1½ CUPS

- ½ baguette, crust removed, torn into small pieces
- 3 garlic cloves
- ⅔ cup blanched almonds, toasted until golden
- 2 large egg yolks, room temperature
- 1 cup extra-virgin olive oil

  Juice of 1 lemon

  Coarse salt and freshly ground pepper

Place bread in a medium bowl and cover with water. Soak until softened, squeeze dry, and crumble until size of large breadcrumbs. Pulse garlic and almonds to a coarse paste in a food processor. Add bread and pulse again until fine crumbs form. Add egg yolks and gradually add oil, pouring in a thin stream while the motor is running, until smooth. Thin with lemon juice. If necessary, add up to ½ cup cool water to achieve desired thickness. Season with salt and pepper.

Anchoïade

MAKES ⅓ CUP

- 16 anchovy fillets, preferably packed in olive oil, coarsely chopped
- 2 garlic cloves, minced (about 1 teaspoon)
- 2 tablespoons extra-virgin olive oil
- 1 tablespoon plus 1 teaspoon fresh lemon juice (from 1 lemon)
- 2 tablespoons finely chopped fresh flat-leaf parsley leaves

  Freshly ground black pepper or red-pepper flakes (optional)

Combine anchovies, garlic, and oil in a small skillet. Cook over medium-low heat, stirring while cooking to crush anchovies into a paste, until anchovies are melted, about 10 minutes. Remove from heat. Stir in lemon juice, parsley, and pepper. Serve warm or at room temperature.

Cucumber Raita

MAKES 1¾ CUPS

1 (10-ounce) cucumber, peeled, seeded, and cut into ¼-inch pieces

1 cup whole-milk yogurt

¼ cup freshly chopped mint leaves

Juice of 1 lime (about 2 tablespoons)

Coarse salt

1 tablespoon vegetable oil

1 tablespoon black mustard seeds

Combine cucumber, yogurt, mint, lime juice, and 1 teaspoon salt in a small bowl. Heat oil in a small skillet over medium. When very hot, add mustard seeds and cook until they pop. Let cool. Add to yogurt mixture and stir to combine. Raita is best served immediately, but can be refrigerated up to 8 hours; drain any liquid before serving.

Cilantro Chutney with Coconut and Lime

MAKES ABOUT ½ CUP

1 teaspoon cumin seeds

6 scallions, white and light-green parts only, chopped

2 small garlic cloves

1 or 2 serrano chiles (seeded for less heat, if desired)

3 cups fresh cilantro leaves

Juice of 3 limes (about ¼ cup)

2 tablespoons shredded unsweetened coconut

½ teaspoon coarse salt

1 tablespoon plus 1 teaspoon extra-virgin olive oil

Heat cumin seeds in a small dry skillet over medium, tossing frequently, until toasted and fragrant, about 1 minute. Let cool slightly, then crush lightly with the flat side of a knife.

Combine scallions, garlic, and chiles in a food processor and pulse until finely chopped, about 10 seconds. Add cilantro, crushed cumin, lime juice, 2 tablespoons water, the coconut, salt, and oil; pulse until a coarse paste forms, about 10 times. Chutney can be made up to 1 day ahead and refrigerated until ready to use. If making ahead, omit lime juice, stirring it in just before serving.

Caesar Dressing

MAKES ABOUT ½ CUP

- 1 large egg
- ¼ cup fresh orange juice
- 2 tablespoons fresh lime juice
- 1 garlic clove, mashed to a paste with a pinch of salt
- ½ teaspoon Worcestershire sauce
- ¼ cup plus 1 tablespoon extra-virgin olive oil

  Coarse salt and freshly ground pepper

Bring a small saucepan of water to a boil. Plunge egg in boiling water 1 minute. Remove from water and let cool slightly (this technique makes for a lighter dressing than traditional Caesar).

Whisk orange juice, lime juice, garlic, and Worcestershire in a large bowl. Crack in egg and whisk to combine. Gradually whisk in oil. Season with salt and pepper.

Smoky Chipotle Salsa

MAKES ABOUT ½ CUP

- 3 garlic cloves
- 4 medium tomatillos (about ½ pound), husked, rinsed, and halved
- 2 chipotle chiles in adobo sauce (from 1 can)

  Coarse salt

Heat a 10-inch cast-iron or nonstick skillet over medium-high. Add garlic and tomatillos. Cook tomatillos, cut-side down, until well browned, about 4 minutes. Turn and cook until tomatillos are completely soft and garlic is browned. Transfer garlic and tomatillos to a blender or food processor, along with chipotles and ¼ cup water. Process to a coarse puree, about 5 seconds. Transfer

to a medium bowl and let cool. Thin with a little more water to desired consistency. Season with salt.

Coleslaw

MAKES ABOUT 6 CUPS

- 6 cups shredded cabbage (about ½ head)
- 2 cups julienned carrots (about 4 medium carrots)
- ⅔ cup mayonnaise
- 2 tablespoons Dijon mustard
- 2 tablespoons white-wine vinegar

  Coarse salt and freshly ground pepper

In a medium bowl, toss together cabbage, carrots, mayonnaise, mustard, and vinegar. Season with salt and pepper. Cover and refrigerate, up to 24 hours.

Pickled Vegetables

MAKES 4 CUPS

- 2½ cups apple cider vinegar
- ⅓ cup sugar
- 2 teaspoons coarse salt
- 4 medium carrots, peeled and cut on the diagonal into ¼-inch-thick pieces
- 2 small red onions, halved and sliced into ¾-inch wedges
- 4 jalapeños, seeded and quartered

Combine vinegar, sugar, and salt in a medium saucepan with 3 cups water; bring to a boil, stirring to dissolve sugar. Add carrots, onions, and jalapeños; reduce to a simmer. Cook until carrots are just tender, 10 to 12 minutes. Pour into a medium bowl; let stand 10 minutes before serving. (Vegetables can be kept refrigerated in an airtight container up to 2 weeks.)

Barbecue Sauces

Whether you're looking for a foolproof barbecue sauce that comes together from your pantry ingredients (our All-Purpose Barbecue Sauce takes just five minutes) or one that has a vinegary punch (ideal for the ribs on page 132), these simple recipes will cover the bases. And don't forget to add the Texas Barbecue Sauce on page 125 to your repertoire, too.

Tangy Barbecue Sauce

MAKES 3 CUPS

- 2 tablespoons vegetable oil
- 1 medium onion, finely chopped
- 3 garlic cloves, minced

  Coarse salt and freshly ground pepper
- 1¼ teaspoons chili powder
- 1 can (28 ounces) whole peeled tomatoes
- ¼ cup packed dark-brown sugar
- ¼ cup ketchup
- 2 tablespoons apple cider vinegar

Heat oil in a medium saucepan over medium-high. Cook onion, garlic, 1 teaspoon salt, and ½ teaspoon pepper until onion is translucent, about 5 minutes. Stir in chili powder and cook until fragrant, about 1 minute.

Coarsely chop tomatoes and add, with their juices, to saucepan. Add ¾ cup water, the sugar, and ketchup. Bring to a boil. Reduce heat, and simmer, partially covered and stirring occasionally, until thickened slightly, about 1½ hours. Add a few tablespoons water, as needed, to avoid scorching. Let cool slightly.

Puree sauce in a blender or use an immersion blender. Stir in vinegar; season with salt and pepper. Let cool. (Barbecue sauce can be refrigerated in an airtight container up to 1 week.)

All-Purpose Barbecue Sauce

MAKES ABOUT 1 CUP, ENOUGH FOR 4 POUNDS MEAT, POULTRY, OR SEAFOOD

- ½ cup ketchup
- ⅓ cup apple cider vinegar
- ½ cup light-brown sugar
- 1 tablespoon Worcestershire sauce
- 3 garlic cloves, minced

  Coarse salt and freshly ground pepper

Bring ketchup, vinegar, sugar, Worcestershire, and garlic to a simmer in a small saucepan. Cook until slightly thickened and reduced to 1 cup, about 4 minutes. Season with salt and pepper, and transfer to a medium bowl.

All-Purpose Basics

This basic rub, marinade, and dry brine all share a common purpose: to highlight the flavors and textures of our favorite grilled foods. Choose a sweet and smoky rub spiked with dried-herbal notes, a bright marinade of garlic and herbs that keeps meat moist, or a formula for dry brine that will never go wrong (it's just salt, pepper, and time).

All-Purpose Rub

MAKES 1¼ CUPS, ENOUGH FOR 5 TO 10 POUNDS OF MEAT, POULTRY, OR SEAFOOD

- ⅓ cup coarse salt
- ¼ cup packed light-brown sugar
- ¼ cup paprika
- 2 tablespoons freshly ground black pepper
- 2 tablespoons dried oregano
- 2 tablespoons dried thyme
- 1 tablespoon cayenne pepper (optional)

In a small bowl, combine all ingredients. When ready to use, sprinkle evenly on meat; let stand uncovered 1 hour, to ensure every bite is well flavored.

All-Purpose Marinade

MAKES ¾ CUP, ENOUGH FOR 2½ POUNDS BEEF, LAMB, CHICKEN, OR FISH

- ½ cup extra-virgin olive oil
- ½ cup coarsely chopped mixed fresh herbs, such as oregano, thyme, savory, flat-leaf parsley, and rosemary, plus more for serving
- 6 garlic cloves, chopped
- Zest of 1 lemon
- ¾ teaspoon coarse salt, plus more for seasoning
- ½ teaspoon freshly ground pepper, plus more for seasoning
- Lemon wedges, for serving

Whisk together all ingredients in a nonreactive dish. Place meat in dish. Rub marinade into meat (no need to do this with fish). Cover dish; refrigerate meat 6 to 24 hours and fish 30 minutes, turning occasionally.

Remove from refrigerator; let meat and marinade come to a cool room temperature. Remove from marinade, letting excess drip off (discard marinade); pat dry with paper towels. Season with salt and pepper.

All-Purpose Dry Brine

MAKES ENOUGH FOR 4 POUNDS MEAT, POULTRY, OR SEAFOOD

- 1 tablespoon coarse salt
- ½ teaspoon freshly ground pepper

Combine salt and pepper, and sprinkle evenly all over meat, poultry, or seafood. Let stand uncovered 1 hour or up to overnight before grilling.

Sweet Additions

While this cake is ideal for warming on the grill and topping with fruit (page 227), it's also a versatile basic: Add a dollop of Greek yogurt or a scoop of ice cream, and dessert is served. Or whip up a batch of gingered nuts to add a crunchy counterpart to almost any dish, whether it's a stone-fruit fool (page 230) or a mellow cheesecake.

Pound Cake

SERVES 12

  Unsalted butter, room temperature

2 cups sifted cake flour, plus more for pan

  Coarse salt

¾ teaspoon baking powder

1¼ cups sugar

4 large eggs, room temperature

1 teaspoon pure vanilla extract

½ cup heavy cream, room temperature

Preheat oven to 325°F. Butter a 4½-by-8½-inch loaf pan; dust with flour. Whisk flour, 1 teaspoon salt, and baking powder in a bowl.

In another bowl, cream 1½ sticks butter until fluffy. Gradually beat in sugar until light and fluffy. Add eggs, one at a time, beating well after each addition. Combine vanilla and cream in a small bowl. Add flour mixture to butter mixture in 3 batches, alternating with 2 batches of cream mixture, beating until combined.

Transfer batter to prepared pan, smoothing top. Bake until cake tester inserted into middle comes out clean, about 1 hour and 25 minutes. Let cake cool in pan

about 10 minutes, then turn onto a wire rack and let cool completely.

Gingered Nuts

MAKES ABOUT 4 CUPS

1 pound unsalted mixed nuts (3 cups)

¾ cup finely chopped candied ginger

¼ teaspoon cayenne pepper

  Coarse salt

2 tablespoons sesame seeds

¼ cup sugar

Preheat oven to 350°F. In a large bowl, combine nuts, ginger, cayenne, 2 teaspoons salt, and sesame seeds. In a small saucepan, combine sugar and ¼ cup water over medium-high heat. Bring to a boil and cook, stirring occasionally, until sugar dissolves, about 3 minutes.

Pour sugar syrup over nut mixture and toss well to combine. Arrange nuts in a single layer on a parchment-lined rimmed baking sheet. Bake, stirring occasionally, until nuts are golden, 15 to 20 minutes. Let cool completely on sheet on a wire rack before breaking into bite-size pieces. Store in an airtight container up to one week.

Photograph Credits

All photography by
Elizabeth Cecil
with the following exceptions:
Aaron Dyer: Page 196
Dana Gallagher: Page 157
Hans Gissinger: Page 99
Ditte Isager: Page 158
John Kernick: Page 44
Ryan Liebe: Page 84
Jonathan Lovekin: Page 216
Johnny Miller: Pages 71, 170
Marcus Nilsson: Pages 23, 75, 88,
115, 161, 187, 195, 219

Con Poulos: Pages 39, 79, 92,
104, 133, 137
Linda Pugliese: Page 12
Andrew Purcell: Pages 96, 192
Sara Remington: Pages 60, 211
Anders Schonnemann: Page 191
Yuki Sigiura: Page 55
Mikkel Vang: Pages 108, 174, 182
Jason Varney: Pages 11, 23, 130
Lennart Weibull: Page 43
Romulo Yanes: Page 107

Acknowledgments

Thank you to editors Susanne Ruppert, Nanette Maxim, Sanaë Lemoine, and Bridget Fitzgerald. Invaluable was Ellen Morrissey, whose ideas and institutional knowledge have always moved mountains. Anna Kovel's culinary expertise and beautiful food styling ensured every recipe both looked and tasted delicious. Photographer Elizabeth Cecil, art director Michele Outland, and prop stylist Megan Hedgpeth masterminded the inviting images. Special thanks to the talented Marcus Nilsson, Kate Berry, and Frances Boswell for the cover, and to the photographers listed above whose work graces these pages.

As always, thank you to Kevin Sharkey, Carolyn D'Angelo, Thomas Joseph, Sarah Carey, and the MSL team for their indispensable input. Other key players include Kavita Thirupuvanam, Caitlin Brown, Pearl Jones, Veronica Spera, Gregory Wright, Denise Ginley, Anne Eastman, Gertrude Porter, Josefa Palacios, Aida Ibarra, Mike Varrassi, Stacey Tyrell, Jeanine Robinson, Alex Kuhn, and Sara and Mott Goodman.

We are pleased to be making books with our Clarkson Potter family, namely Jennifer Sit, Marysarah Quinn, Linnea Knollmueller, Terry Deal, Jennifer Wang, Mark McCauslin, Catherine Casalino, Aaron Wehner, Doris Cooper, Kate Tyler, Stephanie Davis, and Jana Branson.

Index

Aïoli
  almond, 242; grilled spring
    vegetables with anchoïade
    and, 58
  basic recipe, 241
  herb, lamb shoulder chops
    with, 90
Almond aïoli, 242
  grilled spring vegetables with
    anchoïade and, 58
Americano, 69
Anchoïade, 242
  grilled spring vegetables with
    almond aïoli and, 58
Antipasto, grilled vegetable, 61
Apricots
  grilled, honey-glazed pork
    tenderloin with, 168
  grilled pound cake with seasonal
    fruit, 227
Artichoke and crusty bread
  skewers, 61
Asparagus: grilled spring vegetables
  with almond aïoli and
  anchoïade, 58

Bacon
  Martha's favorite cheeseburgers
    with, 117
  turkey-and-bacon burgers, 118
Balsamic-marinated hanger
  steak, 97
Balsamic-orange glaze, grilled kale
  and radicchio with, 194
Bánh mì, tofu, 143
Barbecue
  all-purpose barbecue sauce, 245
  classic pulled-pork sandwiches,
    131
  smoked-brisket sandwiches with
    Texas barbecue sauce, 124–25
  tangy barbecue sauce, 245; grilled
    ribs with, 132
Basil
  basil French 75, 69
  basil, lime, and chile filling, for
    whole grilled fish, 106
  peach panzanella, 197
Beans
  fava: grilled spring vegetables with
    almond aïoli and anchoïade, 58
  fire-roasted rajas tacos with, 151
  potato and green bean salad, 193
Beef, 26, 30, 31. See also Meat
  balsamic-marinated hanger
    steak, 97
  chile-rubbed flank steak tacos, 144

Korean short ribs, 152
Martha's favorite cheeseburgers,
  117
porterhouse steaks with paprika
  potatoes and lemony romaine
  wedges, 167
rib-eye with jalapeño butter, 94
sirloin and vegetable kebabs, 98
sirloin skewers with zucchini, mint,
  and rice, 171
smoked-brisket sandwiches,
  124–25
steak and charred-tomato
  sandwiches, 136
steakhouse burgers, 114
Beer cocktails, 70
Bell peppers. See Peppers
Berries
  berry fizz float, 217
  fresh-strawberry sauce, 224
  grilled pound cake with seasonal
    fruit, 227
  summer-fruit cream pie, 232–33
Bocconcini and tomato skewers, 61
Bok choy
  baby bok choy slaw, 200
  ginger-soy pork chops with, 164
Bourbon
  bourbon mint tea, 69
  vanilla-bourbon butterscotch, 224
Bread. See also Sandwiches
  artichoke and crusty bread
    skewers, 61
  crostini, grilled fresh sardines
    with, 49
  grilled bread and chiles with
    burrata, 62
  peach panzanella, 197
Brined meats and poultry
  all-purpose dry brine, 246
  buttermilk-and-rosemary brined
    chicken, 78
  chicken with green chile
    dressing, 82
  honey-brined chicken wings, 37
  peppercorn-brined pork chops, 86
Brownie sundae ice-cream cake,
  220–21
Bulgur and grilled ratatouille salad,
  209
Burgers, 30
  cheeseburgers, Martha's favorite,
    117
  chickpea and lamb sliders, 122
  lemongrass pork burgers in
    lettuce cups, 128
  steakhouse burgers, 114

turkey, all-time favorite, 121
turkey-and-bacon, 118
Burrata, grilled bread and chiles
  with, 62
Butter
  fennel-shallot, grilled oysters
    with, 46
  jalapeño, rib-eye with, 94
  orange-herb, salmon fillets with,
    101
Buttermilk-and-rosemary brined
  chicken, 78
Butterscotch, vanilla-bourbon, 224

Cabbage
  coleslaw, 244
  and radish slaw, with peanut
    dressing, 201
  shredded, fish tacos with, 147
Caesar dressing, 244
Caesar salad with mojo-marinated
  shrimp, 179
Cake
  brownie sundae ice-cream cake,
    220–21
  pound cake, 247; grilled, with
    seasonal fruit, 227
Capers: Sicilian oregano-caper
  sauce, swordfish with, 102
Celery, potato, and onion skewers, 61
Chamomile tea and limeade, 74
Charcoal, 21
Charcoal grills, 17, 18, 22, 25, 33. See
  also Grilling basics
Cheese. See also specific types
  grilled bread and chiles with
    burrata, 62
  grilled halloumi and vegetables
    with smoky-tomato dressing,
    185
  grilled peaches and figs with
    prosciutto and Robiola, 65
  tomato and bocconcini
    skewers, 61
Cherry beer, 70
Chicken, 26, 30, 78
  all-purpose rub and marinade
    for, 246
  buttermilk-and-rosemary
    brined, 78
  chicken and pea salad with Dijon
    vinaigrette, 156
  chicken and vegetable kebabs, 85
  with cucumber, radish, and cherry
    tomato relish, 160
  dry brine for, 246
  with green chile dressing, 82

grilled sausage and, with leeks, shallots, and onions, 159

sandwiches, bistro-style, 135

satay, 57

spatchcocked, lemon-herb, 81

wings, honey-brined, 37

Chickpea and lamb sliders, 122

Chile(s). *See also* Peppers

basil, lime, and chile filling, for whole grilled fish, 106

chile-rubbed flank steak tacos, 144

chopped-chile relish, 239

citrus-chile turkey breast, 163

fire-roasted rajas tacos with beans, 151

green chile dressing, chicken with, 82

grilled bread and, with burrata, 62

grilled pork tacos al pastor, 148

jalapeño butter, rib-eye with, 94

pickled vegetables, 244

smoky chipotle salsa, 244

sweet and spicy grilled shrimp, 105

whole fish with potatoes, fennel, and, 183

Chimichurri, 238

sirloin and vegetable kebabs with, 98

Chocolate

brownie sundae ice-cream cake, 220–21

dark-chocolate ice pops, 214

hot fudge sauce, 224

white-chocolate ice pops, 214

Chorizo

pork and chorizo kebabs, 89

shishito peppers and, 50

Chowder, clam, striped bass with, 176

Chutney, cilantro, with coconut and lime, 243

lamb kebabs with naan, raita, and, 172

Cilantro

chutney, with coconut and lime, 243; lamb kebabs with naan, raita, and, 172

ginger-cilantro sauce, tofu with, 110

green chile dressing, chicken with, 82

orange-herb butter, salmon fillets with, 101

shrimp with lime, peanuts, and, 45

Citrus-chile turkey breast, 163

Clam chowder, striped bass with, 176

Cocktails. *See* Drinks

Coconut, cilantro chutney with lime and, 243

Coleslaw, 244. *See also* Slaw

Corn

citrus-chile turkey breast with, 163

grilled corn, mint, and scallion salad, 198

striped bass with clam chowder, 176

Couscous and grilled ratatouille salad, 209

Cream

grilled stone-fruit fool, 230

whipped, lightly sweetened, 221

Cream pie, summer-fruit, 232–33

Croutons, polenta, grilled romaine and radicchio with, 210

Cucumbers

cucumber, radish, and cherry tomato relish, chicken with, 160

cucumber raita, 243

peach panzanella, 197

yogurt-cucumber dressing, 239

Curd, lime, 224

Curry

lamb kebabs with naan, cilantro chutney, and raita, 172

red-curry salmon bites, 53

Desserts, 212–35

berry fizz float, 217

brownie sundae ice-cream cake, 220–21

dark or white chocolate ice pops, 214

grilled stone-fruit fool, 230

lemon and mint or watermelon Campari granita, 229

peach sherbet and sorbet, 218

pound cake, 247; grilled, with seasonal fruit, 227

summer-fruit cream pie, 232–33

sundae sauces, 224

Dill-and-lemon filling, for whole grilled fish, 106

Dressings. *See* Sauces and dressings

Drinks, 69–75

Americano, 69

basil French 75, 69

beer cocktails, 70

berry fizz float, 217

bourbon mint tea, 69

iced teas, 74

three sangrias, 73

upside-down martini, 69

Dry brine, all-purpose, 246

Eggplant

and bell pepper skewers, 61

grilled ratatouille and bulgur salad, 209

lamb kebabs with naan, cilantro chutney, raita, and, 172

and tomato, grilled, soba salad with, 186

Eggs, salmon salad with sugar snap peas, new potatoes, and, 175

Farro

and grilled ratatouille salad, 209

with zucchini, pine nuts, and lemon zest, 205

Fava beans: grilled spring vegetables with almond aïoli and anchoïade, 58

Fennel

fennel-shallot butter, grilled oysters with, 46

grilled halloumi cheese and vegetables with smoky-tomato dressing, 185

Sardinian tomato salad, 206

sea scallops over shallot-herb pasta with, 180

whole fish with potatoes, chiles, and, 183

Feta cheese: watermelon, orange, and feta salad, 190

Figs, grilled peaches and, with prosciutto and Robiola, 65

Fish, 30–31, 106

all-purpose rub and marinade for, 246

dry brine for, 246

fresh sardines with crostini, 49

New England fish sandwiches, 139

red-curry salmon bites, 53

salmon fillets with orange-herb butter, 101

salmon salad with sugar snap peas, eggs, and new potatoes, 175

salmon sandwiches with herbed mayonnaise, 140

striped bass with clam chowder, 176

swordfish with Sicilian oregano-caper sauce, 102

tacos, with shredded cabbage, 147

whole, with potatoes, chiles, and fennel, 183

whole, with two herb fillings, 106

Float, berry fizz, 217

Focaccia, Italian sausages and tomatoes on, 41

Fool, grilled stone-fruit, 230

French 75, basil, 69

Fruit. *See also* Berries; *specific fruits*

fruit granitas, 229

grilled stone-fruit fool, 230

sangrias, 73

seasonal, grilled pound cake with, 227

Garlic, leg of lamb with mint and, 93
Garlic scapes: grilled spring
    vegetables with almond aïoli
    and anchoïade, 58
Gas grills, 17–18, 21, 22, 25, 33. See
    also Grilling basics
Ginger-cilantro sauce, tofu with, 110
Gingered nuts, 247
    grilled stone-fruit fool with, 230
Ginger-soy pork chops with bok
    choy, 164
Graham cracker crust, 233
Granita
    lemon and mint, 229
    watermelon Campari, 229
Grapefruit juice, rooibos tea and, 74
Green bean and potato salad, 193
Grilling basics, 14–33
    cleaning the grill, 15, 22, 33
    cooking tips and techniques, 15,
        25, 30–31
    fuels, 18, 21
    gauging doneness, 26, 30, 31
    gauging the heat, 25
    golden rules, 15
    grill types, 16–18
    lighting a fire, 22
    tools, 28–29

Halloumi cheese and vegetables
    with smoky-tomato dressing,
    185
Herbs. See also specific types
    chimichurri, 238
    grilled whole fish with two herb
        fillings, 106
    herb aïoli, lamb shoulder chops
        with, 90
    herbed mayonnaise, salmon
        sandwiches with, 140
    lemon-herb spatchcocked
        chicken, 81
    mixed herb sauce, grilled lobster
        with, 109
    salsa verde, 241
    shallot-herb pasta, sea scallops
        over, 180
Honey-brined chicken wings, 37
Honey-glazed pork tenderloin with
    grilled apricots, 168
Hot fudge sauce, 224

Ice cream
    berry fizz float, 217
    brownie sundae ice-cream cake,
        220–21
    sauces for, 224
Iced teas, 74
Ice pops, dark or white chocolate,
    214

Italian sausages and tomatoes on
    focaccia, 41

Jalapeños. See also Chile(s)
    jalapeño butter, rib-eye with, 94
    pickled vegetables, 244
Jasmine tea and orange juice, 74

Kale and radicchio, grilled, with
    balsamic-orange glaze, 194
Kebabs and skewers
    artichoke and crusty bread, 61
    charred okra with paprika and
        fresh thyme, 54
    chicken and vegetable, 85
    chicken satay, 57
    eggplant and bell pepper, 61
    kofta kebabs, 42
    lamb, kebabs with naan, cilantro
        chutney, and raita, 172
    pork and chorizo, 89
    potato, celery, and onion, 61
    red-curry salmon bites, 53
    scallion and mushroom, 61
    shishito peppers and chorizo, 50
    sirloin and vegetable, 98
    sirloin, with zucchini, mint, and
        rice, 171
    tomato and bocconcini, 61
Kielbasa bites with potato salad, 38
Kofta kebabs, 42
Korean short ribs, 152

Lamb, 26. See also Meat
    chickpea and lamb sliders, 122
    kebabs, with naan, cilantro
        chutney, and raita, 172
    kofta kebabs, 42
    leg of, with garlic and mint, 93
    shoulder chops, with herb aïoli, 90
Lebanese tomato sauce, 239
Leeks, grilled chicken and sausage
    with shallots, onions, and, 159
Lemon(s)
    dill-and-lemon filling, for whole
        grilled fish, 106
    farro with zucchini, pine nuts,
        and, 205
    lemon and mint granita, 229
    lemon-herb spatchcocked
        chicken, 81
    lemon shandy, 70
Lemongrass pork burgers in lettuce
    cups, 128
Lime
    basil, lime, and chile filling, for
        whole grilled fish, 106
    chamomile tea and limeade, 74
    cilantro chutney with coconut
        and, 243

lime curd, 224
lime shandy, 70
Lobster, with mixed herb sauce, 109

Mains, 76–111. See also Platters
    balsamic-marinated hanger
        steak, 97
    buttermilk-and-rosemary brined
        chicken, 78
    chicken and vegetable kebabs, 85
    chicken with green chile
        dressing, 82
    grilled lobster with mixed herb
        sauce, 109
    grilled whole fish with two herb
        fillings, 106
    lamb shoulder chops with herb
        aïoli, 90
    leg of lamb with garlic and mint, 93
    lemon-herb spatchcocked
        chicken, 81
    peppercorn-brined pork chops, 86
    pork and chorizo kebabs, 89
    rib-eye with jalapeño butter, 94
    salmon fillets with orange-herb
        butter, 101
    sirloin and vegetable kebabs, 98
    sweet and spicy grilled shrimp, 105
    swordfish with Sicilian oregano-
        caper sauce, 102
    tofu with ginger-cilantro sauce, 110
Marinade, all-purpose, 246
Martini, upside-down, 69
Mayonnaise. See also Aïoli
    herbed, salmon sandwiches with,
        140
Meat. See also specific types
    all-purpose rub and marinade
        for, 246
    dry brine for, 246
    gauging doneness and target
        temperatures, 26
    grilling tips and techniques, 30–31
Mint
    bourbon mint tea, 69
    grilled corn, mint, and scallion
        salad, 198
    leg of lamb with garlic and, 93
    lemon and mint granita, 229
    salsa verde, 241
    sirloin skewers with zucchini, rice,
        and, 171
    white sangria, 73
Mojo-marinated shrimp, Caesar
    salad with, 179
Mozzarella: tomato and bocconcini
    skewers, 61
Mushrooms
    chicken and vegetable kebabs, 85
    grilled halloumi cheese and

vegetables with smoky-tomato dressing, 185
scallion and mushroom skewers, 61

New England fish sandwiches, 139
Noodles
sea scallops over shallot-herb pasta, 180
soba salad with grilled eggplant and tomato, 186
Nuts, gingered, 247
grilled stone-fruit fool with, 230

Okra, charred, with paprika and fresh thyme, 54
Olives
Sardinian tomato salad, 206
tapenade, 237
Onion(s). See also Scallion(s)
chicken and vegetable kebabs, 85
fire-roasted rajas tacos with beans, 151
grilled chicken and sausage with leeks, shallots, and, 159
grilled halloumi cheese and vegetables with smoky-tomato dressing, 185
grilled ratatouille and bulgur salad, 209
grilled spring vegetables with almond aïoli and anchoïade, 58
pickled vegetables, 244
porterhouse steaks with paprika potatoes, lemony romaine wedges, and, 167
potato, celery, and onion skewers, 61
Sardinian tomato salad, 206
sirloin and vegetable kebabs, 98
Orange(s)
balsamic-orange glaze, grilled kale and radicchio with, 194
jasmine tea and orange juice, 74
mojo-marinated shrimp, Caesar salad with, 179
orange-herb butter, salmon fillets with, 101
Sardinian tomato salad, 206
watermelon, orange, and feta salad, 190
Oregano-caper sauce, Sicilian, swordfish with, 102
Oysters, grilled, with fennel-shallot butter, 46

Panzanella, peach, 197
Paprika
potatoes, porterhouse steaks with lemony romaine wedges and, 167
rouille, 238

Parmesan, farro with zucchini, pine nuts, lemon zest, and, 205
Pasta
shallot-herb, sea scallops over, 180
soba salad with grilled eggplant and tomato, 186
Peaches
grilled figs and, with prosciutto and Robiola, 65
peach panzanella, 197
peach sherbet or sorbet, 218
summer-fruit cream pie, 232–33
in syrup, 233
Peanut(s)
dressing, cabbage and radish slaw with, 201
sauce, chicken satay with, 57
shrimp with cilantro, lime, and, 45
sugared, brownie sundae ice-cream cake with, 220–21
Peas
chicken and pea salad with Dijon vinaigrette, 156
salmon salad with sugar snap peas, eggs, and new potatoes, 175
Peppercorn-brined pork chops, 86
Peppers. See also Chile(s)
eggplant and bell pepper skewers, 61
grilled bread and chiles with burrata, 62
romesco sauce, 241
shishito peppers and chorizo, 50
sirloin and vegetable kebabs, 98
Pie: summer-fruit cream pie, 232–33
Pineapple, charred, grilled pork tacos al pastor with, 148
Pine nuts, farro with zucchini, lemon zest, and, 205
Platters, 154–86
Caesar salad with mojo-marinated shrimp, 179
chicken and pea salad with Dijon vinaigrette, 156
chicken with cucumber, radish, and cherry tomato relish, 160
citrus-chile turkey breast with corn, 163
ginger-soy pork chops with bok choy, 164
grilled chicken and sausage with leeks, shallots, and onions, 159
grilled halloumi cheese and vegetables with smoky-tomato dressing, 185
honey-glazed pork tenderloin with grilled apricots, 168
lamb kebabs with naan, cilantro chutney, and raita, 172

porterhouse steaks with paprika potatoes and lemony romaine wedges, 167
salmon salad with sugar snap peas, eggs, and new potatoes, 175
sea scallops over shallot-herb pasta, 180
sirloin skewers with zucchini, mint, and rice, 171
soba salad with grilled eggplant and tomato, 186
striped bass with clam chowder, 176
whole fish with potatoes, chiles, and fennel, 183
Polenta croutons, grilled romaine and radicchio with, 210
Pork, 26, 31. See also Bacon; Meat; Prosciutto; Sausage
classic pulled pork sandwiches, 131
ginger-soy pork chops with bok choy, 164
grilled pork tacos al pastor, 148
grilled ribs with tangy barbecue sauce, 132
honey-glazed tenderloin with grilled apricots, 168
lemongrass pork burgers in lettuce cups, 128
peppercorn-brined chops, 86
pork and chorizo kebabs, 89
Potato(es)
and green bean salad, 193
paprika, porterhouse steaks with lemony romaine wedges and, 167
potato, celery, and onion skewers, 61
salad, kielbasa bites with, 38
salmon salad with sugar snap peas, eggs, and, 175
whole fish with chiles, fennel, and, 183
Poultry. See Chicken; Turkey
Pound cake, 247
grilled, with seasonal fruit, 227
Prosciutto, grilled peaches and figs with Robiola and, 65
Pulled pork sandwiches, classic, 131

Radicchio
grilled halloumi cheese and vegetables with smoky-tomato dressing, 185
grilled romaine and, with polenta croutons, 210
and kale, grilled, with balsamic-orange glaze, 194

Radish(es)
and cabbage slaw, with peanut
dressing, 201
cucumber, radish, and cherry
tomato relish, chicken with,
160
Raita, cucumber, 243
lamb kebabs with naan, cilantro
chutney, and, 172
Rajas: fire-roasted rajas tacos with
beans, 151
Ratatouille, grilled, in bulgur salad,
209
Red-curry salmon bites, 53
Red peppers. *See* Peppers
Relish. *See also* Sauces and
dressings
chopped-chile, 239
cucumber, radish, and cherry
tomato, chicken with, 160
Ribs
grilled spareribs with tangy
barbecue sauce, 132
Korean short ribs, 152
Rice
ginger-soy pork chops with bok
choy and, 164
sirloin skewers with zucchini, mint,
and, 171
Robiola, grilled peaches and figs
with, 65
Romaine
grilled radicchio and, with polenta
croutons, 210
lemony romaine wedges,
porterhouse steaks with paprika
potatoes and, 167
Romesco sauce, 241
Rooibos tea and grapefruit, 74
Rosemary: buttermilk-and-rosemary
brined chicken, 78
Rouille, 238
Rub, all-purpose, 246

Salad(s)
baby bok choy slaw, 200
cabbage and radish slaw with
peanut dressing, 201
Caesar, with mojo-marinated
shrimp, 179
chicken and pea, with Dijon
vinaigrette, 156
coleslaw, 244
farro with zucchini, pine nuts, and
lemon zest, 205
grilled corn, mint, and scallion,
198
grilled ratatouille and bulgur, 209
grilled romaine and radicchio with
polenta croutons, 210

lemony romaine wedges,
porterhouse steaks with paprika
potatoes and, 167
potato, kielbasa bites with, 38
salmon, with sugar snap peas,
eggs, and new potatoes, 175
soba, with grilled eggplant and
tomato, 186
tomato, Sardinian, 206
watermelon, orange, and feta, 190
Salmon
fillets, with orange-herb butter,
101
red-curry salmon bites, 53
salad, with sugar snap peas, eggs,
and potatoes, 175
sandwiches, with herbed
mayonnaise, 140
Salsa
smoky chipotle, 244
tomatillo, 144
Salsa verde, 241
Sandwiches. *See also* Bread; Burgers
chicken, bistro-style, 135
Italian sausages and tomatoes on
focaccia, 41
New England fish sandwiches, 139
pulled pork, classic, 131
salmon, with herbed mayonnaise,
140
smoked-brisket, 124–25
steak and charred-tomato, 136
tofu bánh mì, 143
Sangrias, 73
Sardines, fresh, with crostini, 49
Sardinian tomato salad, 206
Satay, chicken, 57
Sauces and dressings, savory
aïoli, 241
almond aïoli, 242
anchoïade, 242
balsamic-orange glaze, for grilled
kale and radicchio, 194
barbecue sauce: all-purpose, 245;
tangy, 245; Texas, 125
Caesar dressing, 244
chimichurri, 238
chopped-chile relish, 239
fennel-shallot butter, grilled
oysters with, 46
ginger-cilantro sauce, tofu with,
110
green chile dressing, chicken
with, 82
herb aïoli, lamb shoulder chops
with, 90
jalapeño butter, rib-eye with, 94
Lebanese tomato sauce, 239
mixed herb sauce, grilled lobster
with, 109

orange-herb butter, salmon fillets
with, 101
peanut sauce for chicken satay, 57
romesco, 241
rouille, 238
salsa verde, 241
Sicilian oregano-caper sauce,
swordfish with, 102
smoky chipotle salsa, 244
smoky-tomato dressing, grilled
halloumi cheese and vegetables
with, 185
tahini sauce, 237
tapenade, 237
tomatillo salsa, 144
yogurt-cucumber sauce, 239
Sauces, sweet
fresh-strawberry sauce, 224
hot fudge, 224
lime curd, 224
vanilla-bourbon butterscotch, 224
Sausage
grilled chicken and, with leeks,
shallots, and onions, 159
Italian sausages and tomatoes on
focaccia, 41
kielbasa bites with potato
salad, 38
kofta kebabs, 42
pork and chorizo kebabs, 89
shishito peppers and chorizo, 50
Scallions
grilled corn, mint, and scallion
salad, 198
scallion and mushroom
skewers, 61
Scallops, over shallot-herb pasta,
180
Seafood. *See also* Fish
all-purpose rub and marinade
for, 246
dry brine for, 246
grilled lobster with mixed herb
sauce, 109
grilled oysters with fennel-shallot
butter, 46
mojo-marinated shrimp, Caesar
salad with, 179
sea scallops over shallot-herb
pasta, 180
shrimp with cilantro, lime, and
peanuts, 45
striped bass with clam chowder,
176
sweet and spicy grilled shrimp, 105
Shallots
fennel-shallot butter, grilled
oysters with, 46
grilled chicken and sausage with
leeks, onions, and, 159

shallot-herb pasta, sea scallops over, 180
Shandies, 70
Shellfish. See Seafood; specific types
Sherbet, peach, 218
Sherry sangria, 73
Shishito peppers and chorizo, 50
Short ribs, Korean, 152
Shrimp
   with cilantro, lime, and peanuts, 45
   mojo-marinated, Caesar salad with, 179
   sweet and spicy grilled, 105
Sicilian oregano-caper sauce, swordfish with, 102
Sides, 188–211. See also Platters; Salad(s)
   grilled kale and radicchio with balsamic-orange glaze, 194
   grilled romaine and radicchio with polenta croutons, 210
   peach panzanella, 197
   pickled vegetables, 244
Skewers. See Kebabs and skewers
Slaw
   baby bok choy, 200
   basic coleslaw, 244
   cabbage and radish, with peanut dressing, 201
Sliders, chickpea and lamb, 122
Smoked-brisket sandwiches, 124–25
Soba salad with grilled eggplant and tomato, 186
Sorbet, peach, 218
Spareribs, grilled, with tangy barbecue sauce, 132
Spatchcocked chicken, lemon-herb, 81
Squash. See Summer squash; Zucchini
Starters, 34–67
   charred okra with paprika and fresh thyme, 54
   chicken satay, 57
   grilled bread and chiles with burrata, 62
   grilled fresh sardines with crostini, 49
   grilled oysters with fennel-shallot butter, 46
   grilled peaches and figs with prosciutto and Robiola, 65
   grilled spring vegetables with almond aïoli and anchoïade, 58
   grilled vegetable antipasto, 61
   honey-brined chicken wings, 37

Italian sausages and tomatoes on focaccia, 41
   kielbasa bites with potato salad, 38
   kofta kebabs, 42
   red-curry salmon bites, 53
   shishito peppers and chorizo, 50
   shrimp with cilantro, lime, and peanuts, 45
Steak(s), 31
   balsamic-marinated hanger steak, 97
   chile-rubbed flank steak tacos, 144
   porterhouse steaks with paprika potatoes and lemony romaine wedges, 167
   rib-eye with jalapeño butter, 94
   steak and charred-tomato sandwiches, 136
Steakhouse burgers, 114
Strawberries
   berry fizz float, 217
   fresh-strawberry sauce, 224
   grilled pound cake with seasonal fruit, 227
Striped bass with clam chowder, 176
Sugared peanuts, 221
Summer-fruit cream pie, 232–33
Summer squash. See also Zucchini
   grilled ratatouille and bulgur salad, 209
   sirloin and vegetable kebabs, 98
Sundaes
   brownie sundae ice-cream cake, 220–21
   sundae sauces, 224
Swordfish with Sicilian oregano-caper sauce, 102

Tacos
   chile-rubbed flank steak, 144
   fire-roasted rajas, with beans, 151
   fish, with shredded cabbage, 147
   grilled pork, al pastor, 148
Tahini sauce, 237
Tangy barbecue sauce, 245
   grilled ribs with, 132
Tapenade, 237
Tea
   bourbon mint tea, 69
   chamomile tea and limeade, 74
   jasmine tea and orange juice, 74
   rooibos tea and grapefruit, 74
Texas barbecue sauce, 125
Thyme, charred okra with paprika and, 54
Tofu, 31
   with ginger-cilantro sauce, 110
   tofu bánh mì, 143

Tomatillo salsa, 144
Tomato(es)
   and bocconcini skewers, 61
   cucumber, radish, and cherry tomato relish, chicken with, 160
   grilled eggplant and, soba salad with, 186
   grilled ratatouille and bulgur salad, 209
   Italian sausages and, on focaccia, 41
   salad, Sardinian, 206
   sauce, Lebanese, 239
   smoky-tomato dressing, grilled halloumi cheese and vegetables with, 185
   steak and charred-tomato sandwiches, 136
Turkey, 26, 30
   burgers, all-time favorite, 121
   citrus-chile turkey breast, 163
   kofta kebabs, 42
   turkey-and-bacon burgers, 118

Upside-down martini, 69

Vanilla-bourbon butterscotch, 224
Vegetables. See also Platters; Salad(s); Starters; specific vegetables
   chicken and vegetable kebabs, 85
   grilled vegetable antipasto, 61
   sirloin and vegetable kebabs, 98

Watermelon
   watermelon Campari granita, 229
   watermelon, orange, and feta salad, 190
Whipped cream, lightly sweetened, 221
White-chocolate ice pops, 214
White sangria, 73
Wood chips, 21, 125
Wood grilling, 18

Yogurt
   cucumber raita, 243
   yogurt-cucumber sauce, 239

Zucchini
   chicken and vegetable kebabs, 85
   farro with pine nuts, lemon zest, and, 205
   grilled ratatouille and bulgur salad, 209
   sirloin and vegetable kebabs, 98
   sirloin skewers with mint, rice, and, 171